THE FOOLISHNESS OF THE MESSAGE PREACHED

D1738251

THE FOOLISHNESS OF
THE MESSAGE PREACHED

An Original Collection of

Soul Food Filled Sermons

Volume One

by

Rev. Dr. Leonidas A. Johnson

Rev. Dr. Leonidas A. Johnson

CRYSTAL FOUNTAIN PUBLICATIONS

DIAMOND BAR, CALIFORNIA

THE FOOLISHNESS OF THE MESSAGE PREACHED
An Original Collection of Soul Food Filled Sermons
Volume One
by Rev. Dr. Leonidas A. Johnson

CRYƧTAL FOUNTAIN PUBLICATIONƧ
A Division of **CRYƧTAL FOUNTAIN MINIƧTRIEƧ, INC.**
P.O. Box 4434
Diamond Bar, California 91765

Cover Graphic Design: Gail Oliver
Cover Art: Gerald and Judy Atkin

Library of Congress Catalog Card Number: 98-93799

ISBN: 1-889561-11-8
ISBN: 1-889561-13-4 (Two Volume Set)

Printed in the United States of America

TABLE OF CONTENTS

CONTENTS

For the message of the cross is foolishness
to those wo are perishing,
but to us who are saved
it is the power
of God.

For
it is written:
"I will destroy the wisdom of the wise,
And bring to nothing the understanding of the prudent."

Where
is the wise?
Where is the scribe?
Where is the disputer of this age?
Has not God made foolish
the wisdom
of this
world?

For since,
in the wisdom of God,
the world through wisdom did not know God,
it
pleased
God through
the foolishness of the message preached
to save those who believe.

For
Jews
request a sign
and Greeks seek after wisdom;

but we preach Christ crucified, to the Jews
a stumbling block and to the
Greeks foolishness.

but
to those who are called,
both Jews and Greeks, Christ the power of God and the
wisdom of
God.

Because
the foolishness of God is wiser than men,
and the weakness of God
is stronger
than
men.

For
you see
your calling,
brethren, that not many wise
according to the flesh,
not many mighty,
not many noble,
are called.

But
God has chosen
the foolish things of the world
to put to shame the things of the wise,
and God has chosen the weak things of the world
to put to shame the things
which are mighty;

and the base things of the world and the things
which are dispised God has chosen,
and things which are not,
to bring to nothing
the things
that are,

that
no flesh
should glory in His presence.

But
of Him you are in Christ Jesus,
who became for us wisdom from God
- and righteousness and sanctification and redemption -

that
as it is written,
"He who glories, let him glory in the Lord."

[1 Cor. 1:20-31]

But
we speak
the wisdom of God in a mystery,
the hidden wisdom which God ordained
before the ages for our glory,
which none of the rulers
of this age knew;
for had they
known,
they
would not
have crucified
the Lord of glory.

[1 Cor. 2:7-8]

This

Book

of Sermons

is Published to the

Glory of the Lord God

and to the memory of the legacy of

soldiers who put their hands

on the gospel plow,

my grandfather,

Rev. Herbert Leonidas Johnson

my father,

Rev. Leon Johnson

my son

Alexander L. Johnson

Rev. Dr. Leonidas Alexander Johnson

PROLEGOMENA

What are Soul Food Filled Sermons?

I employ the terms *Soul Food Filled Sermons, Soul Sermons,* and *Soul Preaching* interchangeably to refer to goal oriented sermon preparation and preaching with a focus on the human soul (mind, emotions, and will). *Soul Food Filled Sermons* blend traditional African-American preaching style with contributions from modern educational psychology. *Soul Sermons* are directed to a people who are caught on the web of computer based information systems technology and who paradoxically stand stranded amiss a rising tide of biblical illiteracy in a world where literates are drowning in an ocean of illiterates and semi-literates.

   Soul Preaching employs much of the traditional African-American preaching element of colorful, poetic diction (which naturally complements narrative style preaching) and the generous use of **M**ovement, **I**magination, **S**ound, (**MIS**).

Philosophical Basis of Ministry

The philosophy of ministry from which *Soul Preaching* springs can be ascertained by setting forth three basic questions to be answered in terms of ministerial outcomes. The three essential question to be considered in ministerial encounters areas follows:

   1. *What does God want us to* **Know**?
   2. *What does God want us to* **Feel**?
   3. *What does God want us to* **Do**?

These three goals must be considered and articulated in this goal oriented philosophy of ministry. These three questions represent the integration of several disciplines into a single philosophy of ministry, elucidated by answering the three above mentioned questions (Know?, Feel?, Do?).

Theological Anthropological Basis

Theologically speaking, man can be thought of as being triune (1 Thess. 5:23):

1. Body
2. Soul
3. Spirit

The human soul can further be divided into three parts:

Soul:
1. *Mind* (Knowledge/Wisdom)
2. *Emotions* (Values/Beliefs)
3. *Will* (Volition/Behavior)

Herein lies the main focus of *Soul Preaching*. Overlaying the critical questions of the philosophy of ministry on the human soul reveals the correlation of areas of ministerial concentration in *Soul Preaching*.

Mind
1. What does God want us to **Know**?

This first question deals with **Orthodoxy**, that is, biblically correct doctrine. *Soul Preaching* aims to teach correct doctrine.

Emotions
2. What does God want us to **Feel**?

This second question deals with **Ortho-affectio**, that is, biblically correct desire, passion, and disposition. *Soul Preaching* aims to instill correct disposition by engaging human imagination and emotion in the preaching phenomena (traditional African-American preaching makes a significant contribution in this area).

Will
3. What does God want us to **Do**?

The third question deals with **Orthopraxis**, that is, biblically correct action, behavior, and practice. *Soul Preaching* aims to change and modify behavior.

The design of *Soul Sermons* includes due consideration of ministerial outcomes as related to the human *mind, emotions,* and *will* (**Know?, Feel?, Do?**). That these three areas are of major significance is indicated in that they represent major divisions of concentration in other contributory disciplines.

Philosophy

Three major categories in Philosophy are:

1. Epistemology (**Know**)

2. Metaphysics (**Feel** - Value/Belief)
3. Axiology (**Do** - Acting)

Behavioral/Soicial Sciences

Three major categories in Behavioral/Social Sciences are:

1. Cognitive Domain (**Know**)
2. Affective Domain (**Feel**)
3. Psychomotor Domain (**Do**)

Information Age and Biblical Illiteracy

For many the information age has resulted in much focus on details at the expense of loosing sight of big ideas. There is also evidence that biblical illiteracy is a growing reality in newer generations. These are two important factors which shape *Soul Preaching.*

    Because of the growth in biblical illiteracy, there is an increasing need to incorporate more Christian Education within the preaching event. However, in general, the goal of Christian Education in a teaching situation focuses on a lesson plan with strong emphasis on specific cognitive goals. With preaching, in general, the goal is to proclaim God's personal messages to a people who present , both individually and collectively, with specific felt needs and who need to hear specific relevant messages from the Lord pertaining their specific situations. How can we balance the primarily narrow, specific cognitive oriented goals of Christian Education with the primarily broad, general ministry goals of the preaching event without prolonging the sermon pass a reasonable length of time ideal for maintaining attention span? How can one craft a sermon without: (1) spending too much time giving background biblical information; (2) confusing the listeners with too much content and too many specific details for ideal memory; and (3) going off on tangents in order to meet the specific felt needs of the various listeners that surface at each particular preaching event and threaten the integrity and general cohesiveness of the basic three point didactic sermon?

The content of the message preached is God given and thus, can not be changed but the preaching form and style, the preaching method can be changed. The gospel message doesn't change but preaching & teaching methods do. What different style of preaching would accommodate the movement of God Spirit best in reaching the biblically illiterate masses with good Christian Education outcomes? Perhaps *Soul Preaching* is an answer. *Soul Preaching* is more narrative in form than didactic, but it may involve a combination of both styles.

The Process - The Craft

In the first technical step in creating a *Soul Sermon* is to prayerfully set the passage/text boundaries, study the passage, and make a historical biblical *text outline*. The text should be exegeted, taking into account the historical context, the language and syntax of the biblical text.

The second step is to ascertain the timeless universal principles and eternal truths from the biblical text outline. In this second step the biblical text outline is converted to a *theological outline* of eternal truths as set forth in the text devoid of historical, cultural, and linguistic barriers.

The third step is to compose a contemporary *sermonic outline* from the eternal truths that have been elucidated in the theological outline. It is imperative that the preacher safeguard the sacred treasures of spiritual truths and pearls of wisdom contained within the text and carefully and faithfully package and deliver them to today's listener with a sense of urgency, relevancy, and sensitivity. These timeless principles must be prepared in the soup of Christian Education for consumption by a people that belong to modern times, culture, and language.

The first phase in the development of the sermonic outline is to identify a main thought or main idea from the theological outline that God wants to communicate to the primary and secondary listeners/audience of the preached message/sermon. For example, the primary audience could be a specific local church congregation and the secondary audience could be individuals that purchase sermon tapes, videos, books, or even those that comprise the Internet Christian Cybercommunity Congregation (or vise versa). The combination of meeting specific Christian Education teaching goals and the general goal of meeting the specific needs of a congregation, both individually and collectively, can easily be achieved through the use of narrative in *Soul Preaching*.

Phase two of the development of the sermonic outline is to identify a popular story or illustration that can serve as a suitable carrier of the timeless biblical truth of the main idea. The story or illustration should not rely on prior biblical knowledge as listeners are assumed to be biblically illiterate. During the story line, one can easily branch off into specific ministry issues that meet felt needs of the many listeners. The preacher than can quicker reenter the story line from these specific ministry tangents without confusing the listener with isolated incoherent details because the story acts as facilitator of coherent thought by maintaining focus and relationship to the big idea.

To illustrate, the *Soul Sermon* may be likened to a *Christmas tree*. The story line serves as the main idea and represents the trunk of the Christmas tree. The specific areas of ministry that need to be addressed for various listeners at any particular preaching event represent the branches of the Christmas tree. As the preacher moves up the tree trunk the preacher may also move out from the trunk story line to deal with these specific personal issues, as led by God's Spirit, and then back to the story line. The spiritual pearls and nuggets of truth that result from this tangential movement in thought represent the decorative ornaments on the Christmas tree branches. Instead of loosing logical cohesiveness by addressing these specific issues these tangential pearls complement the main idea and aid in memory of details within the message. Its easy to remember details as long as there is a big picture on which these details can cling. The information age has caused our society to become so detail oriented to the point that details have obscured our ability to see and function with respect to the big picture. The movement through the story line is a movement toward the top of the Christmas tree, completed by celebrating the crowing of the tree with The Bright and Morning Star. Too often sermons are ineffective in the area of teaching Christian Education because the listener-learner is not given a proper reference point from whence to view, categorize, and file the details given by the preacher-teacher.

Phase three of the development of the sermonic outline is to write the sermon. Use the sermonic outline as a guide, but do not limit yourself to it or hindering the Holy Spirit from moving you in new areas of thought and development as the sermon takes final form. Even after the sermon is fully written out in final form, the actual preached message may vary because the spontaneous and dynamic movement of God's Spirit in the preacher-teacher, listener-learner, and preaching-learning environment breaths life into the preaching event and causes each event to be a uniquely different living phenomena.

Learning Styles

Narrative style preaching easily accommodates various learning styles. Three major learning styles are:

1. Visual (Primarily sense - Vision)
2. Auditory (Primary sense - Hearing)
3. Kinesthetic (Primary sense - Touch)
   Note: Significant learning through
   the senses of taste and smell can
   occur pyschogenically, but this
   may not be common.

The use of stories can support each of these learning styles as well as stimulate Imagination and emotion. The preacher-teacher's use of movement, play acting, gestures, and animation during the preaching event gives the visual learner not only the opportunity to snap mental photographs, pictures worth a thousand words, but also the chance to retrieve these mental images and the information associated with them. Fluctuating the voice and the deliberate and skillful use of Sound helps the auditory learner by leaving distinct aural patterns on the mind's neural tape recorder that are readily recoverable by the auditory learner when the mental replay button is depressed. Involving the listener in bodily movements like clapping or waving hands, standing, stomping on the floor, turning to their neighbor, helps to plant valuable memories in the mind of the kinesthetic leaner who's mental alertness is heighten by physical Movement and activity.

The preacher-teacher can help the precious memories of a preaching event linger by utilizing and stimulating as many of the five senses in the listener-learner as possible during the preaching event. Using as many of the five sense as possible helps the learner-listener in the leaning process and therefore helps to achieve positive Christian Education outcomes. It also helps to create a positive leaning experience for the listener who may be bent toward a decreased attention span due to our assimilation into a fast paced, modern, multi-media and entertainment oriented, sensory overloaded, hedonistic, society.

Calvary's Hill-and-Resurrection Sunday

Traditionally, many African-American preachers do not feel they have truly preached unless they tell the "old" story of the Savior's blood, the Savior who died to set us free. It is thought that preaching is not complete unless the preacher walks up Calvary's Hill and rallies the listeners in the *call-and-response* fashion of traditional African-American preaching to a glorious celebration of resurrection of The Bright and Morning Star, *early*, Sunday morning. Typically this occurs at the end of the sermon but is not limited to such a station.

Indeed, is not the basis for miraculous life changing power centered in the "old" historically correct story that Jesus died, was buried, and rose from the dead? Does not this "old" story bear testimony that there is power, wisdom, and hope in the gospel message preached? Is not this central truth, the death , burial, and resurrection of Jesus Christ, not celebrated each Sunday? Was not Communion and Baptism instituted by the Chief Shepherd, the Great Head of the church, to remind us of this central truth? The death burial and resurrection of Jesus Christ is the heart of the *Good News*! Because He lives, we can face tomorrow, all fear is gone, and life is worth the living, just because He lives! Because Jesus lives, every thing, every situation, and every body is subject to His domain, His authority, and His rule. Jesus makes the difference. And to top this news off is the fact that Jesus loves us! I don't know why He loves us. I don't even know why He cares. I don't know why He sacrificed His life to save us, Oh but I'm glad, so glad that He did! Hallelujah! Praise God! That's some good news! What a message! That's the gospel message preached!

Therefore, it is not anything to be frowned upon when a preacher tells this same "old" story at each preaching event. In fact, it is the duty of the preacher to tell this same "old" story over and over and over again. That what God hired you to do. Don't you like your job? Even if you were to approach the pulpit with the *feeling* that God has not given you a specific message to preach, you should *know* that God has hired you to tell the "old" story over and over and over again. Do your job!

Now, when the listener and preacher mutually interact with each other in submission to the movement of the Spirit of God in the preaching phenomena, the drama of worship often results with a personal and glorious encounter of the soul (mind, emotions, will) with the God of Life. This celebration in the soul may be evidenced by outward emotional and/or physical indicators throughout the sermon, but due to differences in personality, disposition, and other character traits, the genuine evidence of this inward encounter with the God of the universe is a change in lifestyle due to increased *trust in* and *obedience to* God. Whether there is an overt emotional response or not, rest assured, the message of the gospel shall *never* loose its power. The preacher should not feel intimidated or hesitant to take the walk up Calvary's Hill at some point during each preaching opportunity (though it may be best fit at the end). This is a path the preacher must trod, be it with the help of the congregation in the *call-and-response* fashion or be it alone. No preacher, worthy to be called a servant of the Most High God, is ashamed to tell the "old" story of the gospel of Jesus Christ.

The *Calvary's Hill-and-Resurrection Sunday* sermon spin-off does not take the place of sound biblically based preaching of the full consul of God. This potentially emotion packed celebration oriented sermon add-on, tag, compliments the cognitive based feast which has already taken place. The celebration may be thought of as a predominately emotion filled dessert. Ideally the key information contained in this add-on segment of the sermon should have already been woven into the fabric of the sermon body.

What Is This Thing Called Preaching?

Who is able to explain what this thing called preaching is all about? It's simple yet complex. Who can understand it? It's a marvelous thing and it's God's doing. The Lord moves in mysterious ways, His wonders to perform. Yes, God works in mysterious ways, His glory to behold!

THE FOOLISHNESS OF THE MESSAGE PREACHED

REFERENCES

Allen, Ronald J. 1995. The Teaching Sermon. Nashville: Abingdon Press.

Anthony, Michael J. ed. 1992. Foundations of Ministry: An Introduction to Christian Education for a New Generation. Wheaton: BridgePoint Victor Books.

Burgess, Harold. 1996. Models of Religious Education: Theory and Practice in Historical and Contemporary Perspective. Wheaton: BridgePoint Victor Books.

Crawford, Evans E. 1995. The Hum: Call and Response in African American Preaching. Nashville: Abingdon Press.

Johnson, Leon and Leonidas A. Johnson. 1996. What is This Thing Called Preaching? An Authentic Collection of Sermons by Rev. Leon Johnson. Vol 1. Diamond Bar: Crystal Fountain Publications.

Johnson, Leonidas A. 1999. Bread of Heaven Songs of Praise:Daily Biblical Devotional Guide Featuring Old Meter Hymns, 2d ed. Diamond Bar: Crystal Fountain Publications.

Massey, James Earl. 1980. Designing the Sermon: Order and Movement in Preaching. Nasvhille: Abingdon Press.

Mitchell, Henry H. 1990. Black Preaching: The Recovery of a Powerful Art. Nashville: Abingdon Press.

Moyd, Olin P. 1995. The Sacred Art: Preaching and Theology in the African American Tradition. Valley Forge: Judson Press.

Pitt-Watson, Ian. 1986. A Primer for Preachers. Grand Rapids: Baker Book House.

Proctor, Samuel D. and Gardner C. Taylor. 1996. We Have This Ministry: The Heart of the Pastor's Vocation. Valley Forge: Judson Press.

Reed, James E. and Ronnie Prevost. 1993. A History of Christian Education. Nashville: Broadman and Holman Publishers.

Robinson, Haddon W. 1980. Biblical Preaching: The Development and Delivery of Expository Messages. Grand Rapids: Baker Book House.

Smith, Sr. J. Alfred. 1984. Preach On! A Concise Handbook of the Elements of Style in Preaching. Nashville: Broadman Press.

Steffen, Tom. A. 1993. Passing The Baton: Church Planting That Empowers. La Harbra: Center for Organizational & Ministry Development.

Stewart, Sr. Warren H. 1984. Interpreting God's Word in Black Preaching. Valley Forge: Judson Press.

Wilhoit, Jim. 1991. Christian Education: The Search for Meaning. 2nd ed. Grand Rapids: Baker Book House.

THE FOOLISHNESS OF THE MESSAGE PREACHED

Chapter 1

The Flintstone Folly

Text: 1 Corinthians 1:17-21

Background: 1 Cor. 3:18-20; 2 Tim. 3:1-7; Hosea 4:6;
             Rom. 1:18-32; 10:2-3

Song: 1. *I'm Going Through, Jesus* (Unknown)

Main Idea: The Gospel message is foolishness to
             the perishing but the wisdom and power of
             God to those who have been saved.

Prolegomena

All praises to God who is the head of my life, to the pastor
of this great church, pulpit ministers, officers, members,
visitors and special guests, it is indeed a privilege to stand
before you today as God's messenger. Please turn with me
to 1 Corinthians 1:17-21. Reading from the New King
James Version you will find these words:

> *For Christ did not send me to baptize, but to*
> *preach the gospel, not with wisdom of*
> *words, lest the cross of Christ should be*
> *made of no effect. For the message of the*
> *cross is foolishness to those who are*
> *perishing, but to us who are being saved it*

is the power of God. For it is written: "I will destroy the wisdom of the wise, And bring to nothing the understanding of the prudent." Where is the wise? Where is the scribe? Where is the disputer of this age? Has not God made foolish the wisdom of this world? For since, in the wisdom of God, the world through wisdom did not know God, it pleased God through the foolishness of the message preached to save those who believe.
[1 Cor. 1:17-21]

The title of this sermon is *The Flintstone Folly.*
Pray.

Sermon Body

There was a television cartoon series produced some years ago by Hanna-Barbera Productions, Inc. called *The Flintstones.* Fred and Wilma Flintstone and Barney and Betty Rubble are the main characters in this fictional cartoon show. I can still remember the song, "Flintstones, meet the Flintstones, they're a modern stone age family...." The term, *modern stone age,* is what I want to call your attention to. This phrase is an oxymoron. According to Webster's New World Dictionary of the American Language (Guralink 1980, 1016) the definition of an oxymoron is "**a figure of speech in which opposite or contradictory ideas or terms are combined.**" For example, like the term *modern stone age* the term, *simply profound, brilliant baffoon,* and *educated fool* are phrases where incongruous, opposite or contradictory ideas or terms are combined. These phrases, these terms, these combinations of words are known as oxymorons.

Something can not be modern and stone age at the same time. Something can not be simple and profound at the same time. A person can not be educated and foolish at the same time. Yet, I have met many a' educated fool in my life, and so have you. Many people sitting in insane asylums may test with a low I.Q. (Intelligence Quotient) but have the potential to function with the genius of an Einstein. Sometimes there is a thin line between being brilliant and being insane. Just because someone is a little eccentric does not mean that they are insane. Many homeless men and women who you may label as being insane are highly intelligent. The idea of this type of oxymoron situation, this contradiction in intelligence and foolishness, is raised in Paramount's popular movie entitled *Forrest Gump* starring Tom Hanks.

Life is often filled with incongruous, contradictory, paradoxical situations and sometimes the best way to describe these odd observations is with oxymorons. For example, America can be said to be a *poor rich* nation. We cry that we are too poor to feed the hungry and take care of the elderly yet we spend millions of dollars on frivolous things. Some juvenile delinquents and law breakers are often described as *good bad* people by law makers. The person who suffers from anorexia or bulimia may believe that she is a *fat skinny* person. The cartoon *The Flintstones* optimizes the juxtaposition of contrasting ideas and contradictory situations described by oxymorons. How can a prehistoric stone age man enjoy modern twentieth century technological inventions? Fred Flintstone drives an automobile. Wilma Flintstone washes dishes with an automatic dishwasher and uses a pig-a-sorus garbage disposal. Barney Rubble calls Fred Flintstone on a telephone about an upcoming bowling tournament sponsored by the Water Buffalo Lodge. Betty Rubble goes grocery shopping at a supermarket and then picks up a dress at the Dry Cleaners. The town of Bedrock has an airport with airplanes that fly to Honolurock. The concept of the cartoon is built around this freak of nature, the odd occurrences in life of incongruous, paradoxical, contradictory realities.

What is the cause of these incongruous, paradoxical, contradictory realities? What is the explanation for these odd occurrences and freak situations in life that give birth to oxymorons. Well, there may be many reasons these situations exist but one reason results from a faulty point of view. There is a folly in perspective. I purpose that many of these rarities in life can be explained. Its a matter of ones point of view. If there is a folly in ones point of view, an error in how one approaches and interprets these oxymoron situations in life, than there is the potential for the emergence of disastrous, life shattering consequences. Many of you are living in an oxymoron situation. Many of you are living in paradoxical, contradictory situations and how you interpret and deal with these situations can have serious, even life threatening, consequences.

Fred was a stone age man yet he was living as thought he was part of our modern day culture with all the conveniences that this age offers. Many of you don't make enough money to buy a can of beans yet you attempt to live as though you can afford to buy whatever your heart desires. This is a paradoxical situation. Many of you dance with the devil on Saturday and sing with the saints on Sunday. You are living a contradictory lifestyle. You are an oxymoron. Turn to your neighbor and repeat these words, "I don't mean no harm, I don't mean to get in your business, but are you an oxymoron?" Turn to your other neighbor and say, "I thought so."

Not only in cartoons, and in our own lives do we see evidence of oxymoron situations but we also see oxymoron statements, phrases, and situations in the Bible.

For example, the phrase *saved sinner* is an oxymoron. If you are a sinner how can you be saved? The penalty for sin is death. According to Gods law, sinners must die. How can you be saved if you are a sinner? The term *Morning Star* is an oxymoron. Stars are seen at night. In the morning the brightness of the rising sun obscures the view of stars. The phrase *the foolishness of the gospel message* is an oxymoron. This phrase implies that the gospel message preached is foolishness. Not so! Not so! Let us focus on this biblical oxymoron today. To approach and interpret this oxymoron in folly, that is, from the wrong point of view, from the wrong perspective, would be disastrous!

The gospel message preached, the message that Jesus Saves, is not foolishness. The gospel message preached is the power and wisdom of an omnipotent, omniscience God. The gospel message is the wisdom of an infinitely wise God. The gospel message is the power of an all powerful God. Why does the wisdom of a God who alone wise and the power of a God who spoke into existence the world and all those who dwell therein seem like foolishness? Why does the gospel message seem like foolishness? Well, all humans were created with limited intelligence by our Creator. There are some things in life we may never understand. Just as though it is impossible for an average three year old to grasp the advance mathematical concepts of astrophysics, there are some things we humans can not grasp about God's universe. The Bible is God's authoritative revelation to humans about what life is all about at a level we can understand. Just because the messages of God have been simplified so that even a child could understand the mysteries of life, do not make the mistake that the message lacks intellectual complexity. To rush to the conclusion that the gospel message is beneath serious consideration and perusal would be a folly. When confronted with oxymoron situations a proper understanding of such conditions demands that we go to Higher source for answers. To do otherwise would be a folly.

On the surface, the Flintstones and other cartoons may seem like a bunch of childhood foolishness yet some cartoons are the result of a great amount of study in the fields of child psychology, educational psychology, music therapy and the use of deductive, inductive and transductive reasoning. Because of what I call the *Flintstone Folly*, some have wrongfully concluded, that the gospel message is foolish. Jean Piaget, the Swiss researcher found that the human mind has a drive to make sense of experiences, thoughts, and feelings (Anthony 1992, 74). There is also a built-in drive toward cognitive stability known as equilibrium (Anthony 1992, 75). **The Flintstone Folly is: (1) the attempt to figure out, on a humanistic level, incongruous, paradoxical, and contradictory situations of a spiritual nature; (2) the humanistic attempt to return to a state of cognitive stability by ridding oneself of cognitive disequilibrium caused by biblical oxymorons.** In other words, man, who is of finite understanding attempts to understand paradoxical and contradictory life situations and/or biblical teachings but instead of seeking the counsel of an infinitely wise God, instead of inviting God to the discussion table, instead of trusting and obeying God who alone is wise regarding such matters, man dismisses God's word and/or rejects God's authority and rule in their personal lives.

The gospel message of salvation is so simple that many refuse to believe it. Many question how something as complicated as eternal life be simplified to matters of love, faith, and hope. Many question how something as complicated as life be simplified to faith in an invisible God. They say life involves molecular biochemical reactions. Life involves organized and sophisticated systems that harmoniously function together. There's the cardiovascular system, pulmonary system, neural system, digestive system, hormonal system, the immune system, skeletal system, how can you reduce life to a matter of love, faith, and hope? All these system must be impacted and must be entered into the discussion of eternal life.

Some say, not only must biological systems be entered into the discussion of eternal life but one should invite natural and physical science to the discussion table. One must take into account Darwin's *Theory of Evolution*, Einstein's *Theory of Relativity*, Stephen Hawking's discourse on *Time*, and the relationships between energy, mass, speed, and the effect forces like gravity have on the aging process. Time travel may be possible if one understands the physical laws and concepts that confines the time space matter continuum in a particular dimensional sphere of existence. Yes, it may be possible to step outside this dimensional sphere and reenter at different point along the artificial time line called human history. Just because humans can not do it dose not mean it can not be done. Therefore, some argue that any discussion of eternal life must include the discussion of the natural and physical sciences, including quantum physics. They ask, "How can you reduce the discussion of eternity to matters of love, faith , and hope?"

Others may raise the question that, "Even if we bypass the scientific topics and jump right into the philosophical discussion of ethics and morality, how can a sinful person who has transgressed the holy righteous laws of God be counted as just and righteous?" What about justification by committing oneself to good works, depriving oneself of fleshly pleasures, and observing the ceremonial laws of Moses? What about human atonement? How can you talk about eternal life without dealing with the philosophical discussion of the moral obligation of the sinner to make amends for the sins committed against a Holy and righteous God?

The Gospel message involves love, faith, and hope and can be summarized in two words, Jesus Saves. A longer explanation would be, by God's Grace through *faith* in Jesus you can be saved from eternal damnation (Rom. 3:23; 6:23; Eph. 2:8-9). Salvation is based on the grace of God. Eternal life is a gift from God. The manner in which we receive this wonderful gift is through faith in Jesus. Its that simple. *For God so loved the world that He gave His only begotten Son, that whoever believes in Him should not perish but have everlasting life* (John 3:16). The basis of the Christian hope is the evidence of an empty grave. The death, burial, and resurrection of Jesus Christ is central to the Christian belief. In essence the message of the gospel preached is that God loves us, that faith in Jesus is the path to eternal life, and that there is hope for a better day. God loves us, God saves us through His son Jesus Christ, and the promises of God are true. The gospel message preached is a love story between you and your creator and this story is filled with **power, wisdom,** and **hope.**

Believe it or not, there is **power** in the gospel message.

Would you be free from the burden of sin?
There's pow'r in the blood, pow'r in the blood;
Would you o'er evil a victory win?
There's wonderful pow'r in the blood.
Chorus:
There is pow'r, pow'r wonder working pow'r
In the blood, of the Lamb;
There is pow'r, pow'r, wonder working pow'r
In the precious blood of the Lamb.
There Is Power in the Blood
(Lewis E. Jones)

THE FLINTSTONE FOLLY

Believe it or not there is **wisdom** in the gospel message.

> I don't worry about tomorrow,
> I just live from day to day.
> I don't borrow from its sunshine,
> For its skies may turn to gray.
> I don't worry o'er the future,
> For I know what Jesus said,
> And today I'll walk beside Him,
> For He knows what is ahead.
> Chorus:
> Many things about tomorrow,
> I don't seem to understand;
> But I know who holds tomorrow,
> And I know who holds my hand.
> *I Know Who Holds Tomorrow*
> (Ira F. Stanphill)

Believe it or not there is **hope** in the gospel message.

> My hope is built on nothing less
> Than Jesus' blood and righteousness;
> I dare not trust the sweetest frame,
> But wholly lean on Jesus' name.
> Chorus:
> On Christ, the solid Rock , I stand
> All other ground is sinking sand,
> All other ground is sinking sand.
> *The Solid Rock* (Edward Mote)

If you don't view oxymoron situations from the right vantage point, then what you see will not make sense to you and you will make assumptions and come to conclusions that are incorrect, and make subsequent decisions that may have a profound effect on your life and

33

your eternal station. When you come up against an oxymoron situation please take a spiritual, biblically based vantage point and get all the facts because if you don't, what you see will not make sense and in order to resolve the intellectual tension that results from paradoxical situations your attempt to bring resolution may lead you down a path of destruction. This is the situation in our text today.

Many intellectuals and religious philosophers had great difficulty accepting the gospel message preached by the Apostle Paul. As a result they concluded that the gospel message was foolishness. This tragic and hasty decision had eternal consequences. The decision not to accept the gospel message is a decision to spend the rest of eternity in damnation with agonizing and tormenting pain.

Salvation is not based on emotional feeling, the church you attend, how many religious conferences you attend, how much money you give to the church, how often you attend church, whether you speak in tongues or not, what denomination you affiliate with, how long you been a member of your local church, how many years you taught Sunday school, how many committees in the church you chaired, what your daddy or mommy did, how you dress, how well you sing, how well you are able to get the church emotionally worked up on Sunday morning, how well you can pray in public, whether you've been baptized by submersion or sprinkled or how smart you think you are. By God's grace through faith in Jesus we are saved from pending judgment of sin and the sentence of eternal damnation. Faith is the key to salvation. Unless we have a childlike faith in Jesus, the gospel message sounds like foolishness to the carnally minded and is a stumbling block to Non-Christian Jews (1 Cor. 1:23).

I don't know about you but I say like Paul, I am not ashamed of the Gospel of Jesus Christ for it is the power of

God unto Salvation for everyone who believes (Rom. 1:16)! Why God decides to use the weak to show Himself strong, why God chooses the simple to confound the wise, why King Jesus was born in a dirty manger may seem like oxymoron situations but **do not** discard the gospel as foolishness because you don't understand how God works. God desires to show himself strong and mighty, wise and able beyond our own abilities. The Lord moves in mysterious ways, His wonders to perform. Yes, God works in mysterious ways, His wonders to behold! He is great and greatly to be praised! Nobody can take His place. There is none like Him. We are the sheep of His pasture. We need Him, He doesn't need us. Yet, even though He doesn't need us He loves us and cares for us. He is merciful, kind and gentle to us. The song writer said, I don't know why Jesus love me I don't know why He cares I don't' know why He sacrificed His life Oh but I am glad, so glad that He did.

Have you made the decision that the gospel message is a bunch of foolishness? Have you heard the message but really do not believe the message? Maybe your are looking at this thing from the wrong perspective. The gospel message is *simple yet profound.* The gospel message preached is an oxymoron! Watch out for parallax and optical like illusions. Just because it does not make sense to you right now does not mean you should discard the gospel message as foolishness. How you deal with this message has eternal consequences. I encourage you, instead of disgrading this message, reconsider it from another vantage point. Maybe you are not ready to make the leap of faith yet, but leap you must in order to be saved. Leap into the hand of Jesus. He'll be there to catch you before you fall. Today is a good day to take that step of faith. Come.

BIBLIOGRAPHY

Anthony, Michael J. ed. Foundations of Ministry: An
    Introduction to Christian Education for a new
    Generation. Weaton,IL: BridgePoint, 1992.

Guralink, David B., ed. Webster's New World Dictionary
    of the American Language. 2d ed., New York:
    Simon & Schuster, 1980.

REFERENCES

Hawking, Stephen. 1988. A Brief History of Time: From
    The Big Bang to Black Holes. New York: Bantam
    Books.

Lefrancois, Guy R. 1994. Psychology for Teaching. 8th ed,
    Belmont, California: Wadsworth Publishing Co.

Chapter 2

The Gingerbread Man

Text: Genesis 3:8; 2 Chronicles 7:14

Background: Genesis 1:26; 2:16-17; 3:1-9;Psalms 95:6-11

Song: 1. *I Will Trust in the Lord*
       (Traditional African American)

Main Idea: Running from God will lead to your
             destruction.

Prolegomena

All praises to God who is the head of my life. To the pastor
of this great church, pulpit ministers, officers, members,
visiting friends, and guest, it is indeed a blessing to be here
today. I want to thank the pastor of this church for
affording me this opportunity to address you.

Lest I hold you too long, if you would be so kind,
turn with me to Genesis 3:8 and 2 Chronicles 7:14. I would
love to tell some of the things God has done and is doing in
my life and how I came to be standing here today but time
is not on my side, time is not my friend today. There is a
word from the Lord that I must share with you and I don't
want to waste any time. Therefore, lets get right to
business. Genesis 3:8 reads as follows:

> *And they heard the sound of the Lord God walking in the garden in the cool of the day, and Adam and his wife hid themselves from the presence of the Lord God among the trees of the garden.*
> [Genesis 3:8]

And over in 2 Chronicles 7:14 it reads as follows:

> *if My people who are called by My name will humble themselves, and pray and seek My face, and turn from their wicked ways, then I will hear from heaven, and will forgive their sin and heal their land.* [2 Chronicles 7:14]

The title of this sermon is *The Gingerbread Man*.
Pray.

Sermon Body

Some of you may be wondering, "What does a children's story and the ancient biblical story of Adam and Eve have to do with me?" That's a good question. I'm glad you asked it. Now if you pray, and pray right, the Holy Spirit will preach, Christ will be magnified, and we all will be edified and blessed. Is that all right?" Amen.

God has an important question that He wants to ask you today. God also wants me to highlight three things from His word that He wants you to know. I'll save these three things for last, so that you won't forget them.

You asked, "What does a children's story have to do with me?" To answer your question, I am going to use a popular and familiar children's story entitled *The Gingerbread Boy* to help you visualize what God is saying to you. There are several versions of this story and I will

38

use my own version of this fictitious story as a mental outline upon which we will navigate through this sermon. It will serve as a mental framework upon which you can hang the individual facts that we uncover from God's word. It will serve as a spiritual coat rack upon which you can hang various scriptures and spiritual truths as they are revealed. This story will serve not only as a vehicle to aid you in processing spiritual information but also as an effective memory device. I understand that most of you have gone to college and many have even completed your masters degree. Several of you even have a doctorate degree. I realize that you are "ed-ja-ba-cated" (educated) and sophisticated. I know that you are beyond Piaget's preoperational stage of cognitive development, but this simple children's story will help us to grasp the essence of what God wants us to know. There are a lot of things that I will be sharing with you but I don't want you to loose sight of the main thrust God' s message.

In addition to the children's story, we will deal with the ancient biblical story of Adam and Eve. You also asked, "What does this story have to do with me?" In reply, unlike the fictitious, human authored children's story which may or may not have any significance in and of itself to you, this biblical story is a true story based on historical fact, authored not by man but by God Himself, and has everything to do with you and me, here and now, and the problems we face from day to day.

"Well," you may ask, "how do these two stories actually meet and intersect with my life and my problems?" Listen up now, this is important. The gingerbread man, Adam and Eve, you and I all have something in common. We all share a common problem. Not only do we all share a common problem, the solution to that problem offers us the key to solving many of the problems we are experiencing in our personal lives, our homes, on our jobs, in the church,

THE FOOLISHNESS OF THE MESSAGE PREACHED

and in society. The solution to this problem gives us a renewed hope that after today we will be filled with the Spirit, that our fellowship with God will be strengthened, that we will be showered with His blessings, that some of our unanswered prayers will be answered, that we will become more fruitful in ministry, that we will be able to praise Him appropriately, that our joy will be restored, and that our spiritual growth will flourish. I have some good news for you today.

"Well", you may ask, "brother preacher, what problem do I have that is common with both the gingerbread man and Adam and Eve?" Are you praying with me?

Gingerbread Man Story to Point of Becoming a Living Being

Let us look at these two stories. In the case of the gingerbread man, there once was a father, son, and a loving, spirited mom. Though they were three, they functioned as one happy family, living in peace and harmony. One day they said, "Let us make a gingerbread man in our image, according to our likeness." And they formed the gingerbread man out of the dust of the ginger with molasses and put him into the oven of creation and the gingerbread man became a living being.

Point of Departure - Story of Adam and Eve to Point of Becoming a Living Being

Now, at this point allow me to depart from the gingerbread man story and deal a little bit with the story of Adam and Eve. In the beginning there was God the father, God the son, and God the Spirit. Though they were three, they were one. One day they said, "Let Us make man in Our image, according to Our likeness." And they formed man out of the dust of the ground, and breathed into his nostrils the breath of life; and man became a living being.

Both the gingerbread man and man were created and became living beings, complete with free wills.

Resume Gingerbread Man Story to Point of all Running After Him

Back to the story of the gingerbread man. The father, son and spirited mom loved that gingerbread man very much. They told the gingerbread man that he was special, that they made him for a reason and purpose and that they had prepared a special place for him to live. But first, he had to sit by the window to cool off. The father warned him and said to him, "Do not go outside for in the day you go outside you will surely get eaten and die." As the gingerbread man sat by the window he looked out and saw a beautiful garden. Out jumped the gingerbread man. He disobeyed the command of his father and creator. When the father noticed that the gingerbread man was gone, He went out looking for the him and called out to the gingerbread man, "Where are you?" When the gingerbread man heard the sound of the father walking near the garden he hid himself among the plants of the garden and fled from the presence of the father.

The gingerbread man ran past a policeman and shouted out, "You can run and run, just as fast as you can, but you can't catch me, I'm the gingerbread man." The gingerbread man ran past a school and shouted out to the teacher, "You can run and run, just as fast as you can, but you can't catch me, I'm the gingerbread man." The gingerbread man can to a hospital and shouted out to the doctor, "You can run and run, just as fast as you can, but you can't caught me, I'm the gingerbread man." The gingerbread man came to a church and shouted out at the preacher, "You can run and run, just as fast as you can, but you can't catch me, I'm the gingerbread man." Repeat after me, "You can run and run..."

Point of Departure - Story of Adam and Eve

At this point, I would like to again depart from the fictitious gingerbread man story and deal with the true story of Adam and Eve. Are you praying? God planted a garden eastward in Eden, and there He put Adam and Eve. And out of the ground the Lord God made every tree grow that is pleasant to the sight and good for food. And the Lord God commanded the man, saying, "Of every tree of the garden you may freely eat; but of the tree of the knowledge of good and evil you shall not eat, for in the day that you eat of it you shall surely die."

> Gen. 3:6-9: 3:6 So when the woman saw that the tree was good for food, that it was pleasant to the eyes, and a tree desirable to make one wise, she took of its fruit and ate. She also gave to her husband with her, and he ate. 3:7 Then the eyes of both of them were opened, and they knew that they were naked; and they sewed fig leaves together and made themselves coverings. 3:8 And they heard the sound of the Lord God walking in the garden in the cool of the day, and Adam and his wife hid themselves from the presence of the Lord God among the

trees of the garden. 3:9 Then the Lord God called to Adam and said to him, "Where are you?"

Adam and Eve disobeyed God and when they heard the sound of the Lord God walking in the garden they fled from the presence of God. They ran from God. They ran in the wrong direction!

Surface Common Problem

Watch this now. The gingerbread man had a problem, Adam and Eve had a problem, you and I have a problem. We all have the same problem. "Well, what problem is that brother preacher?" **We all have the problem of not only disobeying the commands of our creator but we are also guilty of running from our creator**. The gingerbread man disobeyed his creator and ran. Adam and Eve disobeyed God their creator and they ran. When you and I disobey God our creator, we run. Its in our sin nature to run from God. Our common problem is that we all disobey the commands of our creator and we find ourselves running in the wrong direction. I see some of you are not convinced yet.

God has created you and me for a reason and purpose. He has prepared a wonderful place for us to live but because of that thing called "free will" we all have gone astray. We disobey God daily. Sometimes we may do what God wants us to do, or say what He wants us to say, or go where He wants us to go, but for the most part, we choose to do what we want to do, say what we want to say, go where we want to go. We often decide to disobey God and live our lives the way we want to live them instead of the way God wants us to live them. We fail to realize that the

43

only way we can be completely satisfied with life and completely fulfilled in life is when we totally submit to God's will in Christ by the power of the Spirit. Remember, the Lord God created you and me in His image and in His likeness. He loves us and wants the best for us. He wants us to be free. He wants us to know the truth. He wants us to live with joy. He wants us to live in peace. He wants to fulfill our every need. Why? Because we reflect His glory, His majesty, His honor, His power, His creativity, His diversity, His ability to make choices as a free moral being. In His likeness, He created us with a free will! We have to make choices in life and deal with the consequences of those decisions. That's part of being made in His image. We choose to disobey God. We choose to disregard His commandments. We choose to move in the wrong direction. If God says go left we go right, if God says go north we go south, if God says love your enemy, we hate our enemy, if God says glory in the Lord, we glory in getting paid. Are you praying?

That brings us to the question that God wants you to consider. God's question to you is, **"Why are you running from Me?"** The reason God is asking you this is because too many of us are running in the wrong direction. Every time we sin, we must choose to either run to God or run from Him. How do you respond when God convicts you of the sins in your life? How do you respond when He lets you know that you are not living right? Do we immediately confess those sins or do we stick them in our secret closet. Are we packing our traveling bags with unconfessed sins? Are we trying to carry the weight of unconfessed sins as we travel through this barren land? Do we have a problem admitting when we are wrong, even to God?

Adam and Eve chose to cover and conceal their sin. Instead of choosing to run to God for help, they choose to run in a different direction. They ran in the wrong direction. They fled from the presence of God.

Resume Gingerbread Man Story to Point of Trusting the Fox

As you may recall, when we last left the gingerbread man he was running. He ran from the policeman, he ran from the teacher, he ran from the doctor, he ran from the preacher. He ran and ran and ran until he came to a river that seemed uncrossable. He turned around and he saw the policeman, the teacher, the doctor and the preacher running toward him. The gingerbread man thought to himself, "I need to get across this river." As he stood on the banks of the river, this old sly fox was checking out the scene.

Point of Departure - Running From God

You know, you and I are just like that gingerbread man. The gingerbread man ran from the police. We run from those who are in authority over us. Children, you need to obey your parents. We run from those who we are accountable to, especially in the church. We have church leaders who act like they don't have to be held accountable to nobody. Even pastors need to be held accountable to someone or some group to help guard themselves against moral failure and unrighteousness. That's one reason why so many pastors of large ministries have fallen into moral sins. We run from humility and submission right into the hands of rebellion and defiance. That's not good. Proverbs 16:18 reads, "Pride goes before destruction, And a haughty spirit before a fall." Perhaps that's an unconfessed sin that

THE FOOLISHNESS OF THE MESSAGE PREACHED

you are harboring in your life. God wants you to deal with that.

I'M TALKING ABOUT RUNNING IN THE WRONG DIRECTION!

The gingerbread man ran from the teacher. We run from those who offer us knowledge, understanding, and wisdom. We disrespect those who labor to teach us. We don't want to do our homework. We don't want to go to school. We don't want to prepare ourselves to be competitive at work. We don't want to learn how to operate computers. We don't want to go to Sunday School or Bible study. The only time some of us open our bibles is when the preacher is giving his text. God is not satisfied with that. 2 Tim: 2:15 reads, "Study to show thyself approved unto God, a workman that needeth not to be ashamed, rightly diving the word of truth." (KJV) We are running from God's word.

I'M TALKING ABOUT RUNNING IN THE WRONG DIRECTION!

The gingerbread man ran from the doctor. We run from those who God has sent to heal us. We want to pray to God for a healing, then we decide not to go to the doctor. That's not right. And if we do go to the doctor, we don't want to listen to the doctor. That's not right. It don't work that way. God uses doctors as instruments of healing. We like to sing that song, Jesus is on the main line, tell Him what you want, if you are sick and can't get well, tell Him what you want. The reason why some of us are sick and can't get well is because we don't want to get well. We have certain lifestyles that we simply do not want to give up. We don't want to change our diet, we don't want to exercise, and we don't want to take our medications. That's not right. No no no, we ought to stop playing with God. He is not happy with us because we are running from the people He uses to help us get well.

I'M TALKING ABOUT RUNNING IN THE WRONG DIRECTION!

The gingerbread man ran from the preacher. We are good about running from the preacher. One reason we run from the preacher is that we expect the preacher to live a perfect, sinless life, and when we see a fault in the preacher, instead of getting up under him and lifting him up before the Lord in prayer, and talking to him, we talk about him, tear him down, and leave the church. That's not right. Are you praying? Another reason why we run from the preacher is that we get mad with the preacher for speaking words of God, words that we don't want to hear. That's not right. The preacher reminds us that we like to act. We profess to be Christians but when the cost of being a Christian comes into play, we transform. We want to lay our religion down and act as though we have amnesia. That's not right. We also run from the preacher not because we are mad with the preacher, but because we are mad with God. We are angry with God because something has happened in our life that we do not understand. Are you praying? Listen, God is too wise to make a mistake and too loving to be unkind. By and by, when the morning comes, you'll understand it better. Stop running from God!

I'M TALKING ABOUT RUNNING IN THE WRONG DIRECTION!

When God convicts of us sin and we choose to cover and conceal that sin instead of confessing that sin, there are spiritual consequences. When God convicts us of sin and we run from God instead of to God, we suffer spiritually. There are eight spiritual consequences of harboring unconfessed sins in the life of the believer. They are as follows:

1. The Holy Spirit is Grieved (Eph. 4:30; cf. filled with the spirit in Eph 5:18)

2. Fellowship is hindered (1 John 1:5-6)
3. Blessings are withheld (Jer. 5:25)
4. Prayers are unanswered (Ps. 66:18; Prov. 28:9)
5. Fruitfulness is hindered (John 15:2-4)
6. Praise is inappropriate (Is. 29:13)
7. Joy is removed (Ps. 51:12)
8. Growth is hindered (1 Cor. 3:1-3)

Resume Gingerbread Man Story to the End

You may recall that when we left the gingerbread man he was on the banks of the river. The policeman, the teacher, the doctor, and the preacher were rapidly gaining on him. Hiding over in the bushes was an old cunning, fox. Well, that fox jumped out and said to the gingerbread man, come on, grab my tail and I will swim you over safely to the other side. The gingerbread man was fast, but not so smart. The gingerbread man said to the fox, you just want to catch me and eat me. The fox said, hurry, they are coming, they're going to catch you if you don't act quickly. Hurry, hurry, grab my tail, I will not eat you. So the gingerbread man grabbed the foxes tail and the fox started swimming across the river. The fox started padding slower and began to sink. The fox said to the gingerbread man, "the water is getting deeper, you better hop on my back." So the gingerbread man hopped on the back of the fox. The fox began to paddle slower and began to sink more. The fox said to the gingerbread man, "You better hop on top of my head, the water is getting deeper." So the gingerbread man hopped on top of the head of the fox. Once again, the fox started to paddle slower and said to the gingerbread man, " The water is getting deeper, hop on top of my nose." When the gingerbread man went to hop on top of the foxes nose, the fox opened up his big mouth and ate the gingerbread man.

Running in the Wrong Direction and Legitimate Needs

The gingerbread man thought he was invincible until he got to the river. He had trouble at the river. I don't know about you but I don't want no trouble at the river. The gingerbread man had a need to get across the river. The gingerbread man sought to fulfill that need by trusting the fox. As a result, he lost his life. Maybe you are doing pretty good in life. Maybe you believe, like the gingerbread man, that you are invincible. My question to you is, "When you come to rivers that seem uncrossable, who will you trust if you are running from the God that specializes in things that seem impossible?" Will you foolishly put your trust in your enemy as did the gingerbread man? Can you even identify the enemies that will offer you help in a time of need?

1. Your first enemy is your flesh. The goal of your flesh is:
   a. For you to live life based upon the impulses of your sin nature.
   b. For you to indulge.
   c. For you to take God's good gifts and distort them into perversion.
2. Your second enemy is the World. The goal of the world is:
   a. For you to buy into the unstable, deteriorating, morally bankrupt value system of our modern day culture and society.
   b. For you to spend your time, energy, and resources man's way.

3. Your third enemy is none other than the Devil. His goal is:

    a. For you to waste your life on useless activity.

    b. For you to destroy your life from counting for God.

    c. For you to take your own life (Physically, Mentally, Emotionally, and Spiritually).

God's Treatment of Sin

How does God treat unconfessed sins in the life of the believer and the non-believer? If you are a believer and you harbor unconfessed sins in your life, in addition to the spiritual consequences already mentioned, God will also discipline you (see 1 Cor. 11:31-32; Heb. 12:5-11). God's discipline for unconfessed sin can led to sickness and, ultimately, physical death (Acts 5:1-11; 1 Cor. 11:30 cf. vv. 23-29, 31-34; 1 John 5:16-17; potential case 1 Cor. 5:1-5). The believer who experiences physical death as a result of God's discipline for their unconfessed sins will still be granted eternal life based on their faith in the person and purpose of Jesus Christ (John 11:25). Why does God discipline us?

    1. Because He loves us (Heb. 12:6; Prov. 3:11-12).
    2. That we may be partakers of His holiness - (Heb. 12:10).
    3. For spiritual growth - to yield the peaceable fruit of righteousness (Heb. 12:11).
    4. For protection - that we may not be condemned with the world. (1 Cor 11:32).

50

If you are a non-believer and you harbor unconfessed sins in your life, you will experience the wrath of God. That means you will not only experience physical death but spiritual death and eternal damnation.

The Correct way to Deal with Sin

God wants you to know three things today. He has asked you the question, **"Why Are You Running From Me?"** Now God wants you to consider three things. He wants you to know the three things that you should do when He convicts you of sin:

1. Immediately confess your sin <u>and</u> repent.
2. Commit yourself to the Lord.
3. Judge yourself.

First, God wants us to immediately confess and repent of our sins to God. We are not to pass over them with the rational that God understands. What He understands is that you don't want to deal with your sins His way. In Proverbs 28:13 God says, "He who covers his sins will not prosper, But whoever confesses and forsakes them will have mercy." (See also 1 John 1:9; Ps. 32.5) Too many of us are accustom to running from our problems. Sin is one problem you can not out run. Every man, woman, boy, and girl is confronted with the problem of sin. When we fail to deal with our sins Gods way, when we practice concealing personal sins, when we run from God, we are headed for destruction.

Second, not only does God want us to confess and repent of our sins but we are to make a new commitment to the Lord (read Ps. 51:8-19).

THE FOOLISHNESS OF THE MESSAGE PREACHED

Third, we are to judge ourselves (see 1 Cor. 11:31). How should we judge ourselves? We should judge ourselves by fasting.

a. The Israelites fasted and repented and put away false gods - 1 Sam. 7:6
b. David fasted and repented of his sin - 2 Sam. 12:16; 21-23
c. Ahab fasted and repented after causing Naboth's death - 1 Kings 21:27
d. Hearing God's Word, Israel fasted, confessing their sins - Neh. 9:1-3
e. Daniel fasted and repented for himself and the people for not having walked in the laws of the Lord - God's chastisement was to come - Dan. 9:3
f. Joel called for a fast because of the Lord's chastening - Joel 1:14; 2:12,15
g. The people of Ninevah repented in fasting - Jonah 3:5

Note: The Bible describes three main forms of fasting:

a. **Normal Fast** which involves the total abstinence of food. Luke 4:2 reveals that Jesus "did eat nothing." Afterwards "He was hungered." Jesus abstained from food but not from water.
b. **Absolute Fast** as seen in Acts 9:9 where we read that for three days Saul (who is also called Paul, see Acts 13:9) "neither did eat nor

52

drink." The abstinence from both food and water seems to have lasted no more than three days (Ezra 10:6; Esther 4:16).

c. **The Partial Fast** -as seen in Daniel 10:3 the emphasis is upon the restriction of diet rather than complete abstinence. The context implies that there were physical benefits resulting from this partial fast. However, this verse indicates that there was a revelation given to Daniel as a result of this time of fasting.

Note: Your decision to fast is personal and should be done in secret. However, if you have any medical conditions or aliments and/or are under any medical treatment, I advise you to discuss your desire to fast with your doctor before fasting.

Conclusion

The gingerbread man exercised his free will and decided to disobey his creator's command and disregarded His creator's design for him in life. The gingerbread man ran from his creator, by the enemy, and got eaten and died.

Adam & Eve exercised their free will and decided to disobey God's will for them in their lives. They hid from the presence of God and as a result death entered into the world and they experienced physical death. You and I must choose to obey God. When we disobey God we sin. When God convicts us of sin we must choose either to cover and conceal our sin or immediately confess it. We either run to God or run from Him. If we are believers and we run from Him we will suffer spiritual consequence and God will discipline us. God's discipline may even lead to sickness and physical death. He disciplines us because He loves us. If you are a non-believer and you run from God, you will experience the wrath of God. If you have never given your life to Christ, you need to do so today.

How do you respond when God convicts you of the sins in your life? Don't make the mistake the gingerbread man made. He ran in the wrong direction. Don't make the mistake Adam and Eve made. They ran in the wrong direction. If you are running from God you are running in the wrong direction. Running in the wrong direction is dangerous. Running in the wrong direction will lead to your destruction. That's no joke, that's for real, and that's a fact. Make the decision today to: (1) confess and repent; (2) commit yourself to Jesus Christ, believers included; and, (3) judge yourself with fasting. If you do these three things, God will bless you.

Do not forget what He has said. He has said:

if My people who are called by My name will humble themselves, and pray and seek My face, and turn from their wicked ways, then I will hear from heaven, and will forgive their sin and heal their land. [2 Chronicles 7:14]

Amen!

Chapter 3

When You Wish Upon The Star

Text: John 15:7-8

Songs: 1. *Standing on the Promises* (R. Kelso Carter)
        2. *I Want to Go to That Distant Land* (Traditional)
        3. *Come on, Come on, Come on* (Traditional)

Main Idea: When you abide in Christ, the Bright and
                Morning Star, dreams do come true.

Prolegomena

> Standing on the promises that can not fail,
> When the howling storms of doubt and fear assail,
> By the living word of God I shall prevail,
> Standing on the promises of God.
> *Standing on the Promises* (R. Kelso Carter)

All praises to God who is the head of my life, to the pastor of this great church, pulpit ministers, officers, members, visitors and special guests, it is indeed a privilege to stand before you today as God's messenger.

During Jesus' earthly ministry Jesus announced, "*the kingdom of heaven is at hand*" (Matt. 4:17) and with regard to the kingdom living Jesus said something very special. Please turn with me to John 15:7. There you will find our text. Jesus said,

If you abide in Me, and My words abide in you, you will ask what you desire, and it shall be done for you. By this My Father is glorified, that you bear much fruit; so you will be My disciples. [John 15:7-8]

I would like to speak topically from the title (subject), **When you wish upon The Star.**
Pray.

Introduction

I have been told of a *distant land* where they say dreams come true. In this magical kingdom they say:

> When you wish upon a star,
> Makes no difference who you are,
> Anything your heart desires,
> Will come to you.
>
> If your heart is in your dream,
> No request is too extreme,
> When you wish upon a star,
> As dreamers do.
> *When you wish upon a star* (Ned Washington)

Surely, a land where dreams come true would be a happy place. While I must applaud Walt Disney for his desire to create such a place here on earth, I can't help but to notice that his dream come true of a land considered by many to be most the happiest place on earth is merely a testimony of a truth revealed in scripture. Spiritual reflection on Disneyland's theme song, "When you wish upon a star" dimly reflects a true message embedded in the Gospel of Jesus Christ.

The natural message of Disneyland's theme song is, when you wish upon a star anything your heart desires will come to you. The song "When you wish upon a star" comes from Disney's full length motion picture *Pinocchio*. According to Jiminy Cricket, one night, Geppetto, an old wood-carver, saw the wishing star. Geppetto quickly repeated the special phrase, "Star light, star bright, first star I see tonight, I wish I may, I wish I might, have the wish I make tonight." In this story Jiminy Cricket testifies that he heard Geppetto tell Figaro, Geppetto's pet cat, he wished that the wooden boy he made and named Pinocchio, would become real. That very night a real live fairy floated from the wishing star into Geppetto's shop. Because Geppetto had lived in such a way that gave so much happiness to others, Geppetto's wish came true. Pinocchio, also had a dream. He told the wishing star fairy that he wanted to be a real boy, not made of wood. The fairy told Pinocchio that in order to become real boy, he had to live in such a way that demonstrated that he was brave, truthful, and unselfish. Pinocchio is the story of his attempt to live that certain way. In the end, Pinocchio is successful and his dream comes true.

The story of Pinocchio is a fairy tale and the Magical Kingdom of Disney is a reflection of the wonderful world of imagination, fantasy and adventure. However, we did not gather here today to talk about fairy tales. No, I want to share with you a word of encouragement from the Lord. The Gospel of Jesus Christ is no fairy tale, it is real. Holy Scripture is based on historical facts, yet there are eternal truths and promises contained in the Bible that are more wonderful than those contained in fairy tales.

THE FOOLISHNESS OF THE MESSAGE PREACHED

Sermon Body

In order for you to hear God's message you must have child like faith and a sense of imagination. Unfortunately, I realize that many of us have lost our sense of imagination and our ability to dream somewhere along life's highway of adversity, misery, and strife. Our way has become dark and dreary because we have internalized discouragement and doubt. History has taught us that once an oppressed people or person internalizes discouragement and doubt, there is no need for chains. When a person looses his or her the ability to **imagine** a better tomorrow, when he or she looses the ability to **dream** of a brighter day, when he or she looses the ability to **visualize** a happy ending, that person has enslaved himself or herself in mental bondage. The internalization of discouragement and doubt clouds the mind, suffocates creativity, and entangles one in a treacherous downward mental escalator ride from hopelessness, to depression, to mental and/or physical suicide. The question remains unanswered, "What happens to a dream deferred?" Have your dreams dried up like a raisin in the sun? Have you lost hope? Has your imagination become as dry bones?

This day I encourage you to dream once again. O dry bones hear the words of the Lord (cf. Ezekiel 37:4). In the name of Jesus I declare that no weapon formed against you shall prosper and every weapon that rises against you, that would prevent you from *imagining* the great possibilities of serving a God who never fails, shall utterly be destroyed (cf. Is. 54:17).

There is a *distant land* where the dew drops of God's mercy shine bright. In this kingdom of God there is a Bright and Morning Star (Rev. 22:16), called the Christ. When you pray to God for the desires of your heart in view of this special star called the Lord Jesus Christ, there is a real basis, not imaginary, for the dreams you dream to come true. I bear good tidings, God is in the business of making dreams come true.

I know it sounds like a fairy tale, a children's story, but it is in the Book. Its in here! Its written in God's word. He said it, I believe it. He said it, it's true. He said it, it's for real. He said it, I'm a witness. Believe it or not!

I realize that many of you may have difficulty with this topic. You may say, this is nothing but hocus pocus, mumbo jumbo, childhood nonsense. Well, I'm not saying you can treat God as though He came out of a magic lamp. No, you are not Aladdin and God is not your personal Genie. I'm not saying you can make a wish, chick your heels three times and wish your way out of your land of Oz, your land of heartache and trouble that you find yourself in as a consequence of your own actions and behavior. No, God does not grant wishes based on your possession of magical slippers. No, religious artifacts, jewelry, amulets, charms, crystals, and other like objects will not make the desires of your heart come to you. No, God does not grant wishes based on your observance and or participation in ceremonies, festivals, and/or rituals. No, God does not grant wishes based on your ability to repeat certain special phrases. No, I'm not talking about putting your trust and hope in no hocus pocus mumbo jumbo stuff. No, I'm not talking about no childhood nonsense.

Well, what are you talking about? I am talking about a biblically based wonderland who's foundation was not made by man. A spiritual kingdom where every knee must bow and every tongue confess that Jesus is Lord. A kingdom where you must be, you got to be born again. A kingdom where the substance of things hoped for can become a reality in your life. I'm talking about a kingdom you can enter today by confessing and repenting of your sins and accepting Christ as your Lord and Savior. I'm talking about an all-powerful, all-wise, loving God who finds delight in making the dreams, hopes, wishes, and desires of His children come true. I'm talking about a God who has recorded in His word, "*Is anything too hard for the Lord?....*" (Gen. 18:14) I'm talking about trusting in the Lord thy God with all your heart and leaning not on your own understanding (Prov. 3:5). I'm talking about Jehovah-Jireh, that's no mumbo jumbo, that means *The-Lord-Will-Provide* (Gen. 22:14). I'm taking about standing on promises that can not fail. I'm talking about putting your faith and hope in Jesus Christ, the Bright and Morning Star!

You may say, "Preacher, if God is in the business of making dreams come true, then why have not my dreams come true?" Well, let us take a careful look at this thing. I've searched the scriptures and discovered that there are at least three conditions we must meet before we can rightfully expect God to honor His word to make the desires of our heart come true.

The first condition that must be met is that, above all, we must seek God. After all, isn't it from God that all blessings flow? Even Jesus said, "*Seek first the kingdom of God and His righteousness...*" (Matt. 6:33). This first condition comes with a guarantee. God's word promises that if we seek God, we shall find Him. Hebrews 11:6 says He is a rewarder of those who diligently seek Him. Deuteronomy 4:26b says, "*...you will find Him if you seek Him with all your heart and with all your soul.*" I Chronicles 28:9b reads, "*...the Lord searches all the hearts and understands all the intent of the thoughts. If you seek Him, He will be found by you;....*" Jeremiah 29:13 reads, "*And you will seek Me and find Me, when you search for Me with all your heart.*" Matthew 7:7-8 says, "*Ask, and it will be given to you; seek, and you will find; knock, and it will be opened to you. For everyone who asks receives,* *and he who seeks finds, and to him who knocks it will be opened."* Hebrews 11:6 reads, *"But without faith it is impossible to please Him, for he who comes to God must believe that He is, and that He is a rewarder of those who diligently seek Him."* James 4:8a reads, *"Draw near to God and He will draw near to you...."* He who seeks the Lord shall find Him. That's why Psalms 105:3b states, *"...Let the hearts of those rejoice who seek the Lord."* Those who seek the Lord can rejoice because they shall find Him. The first condition is to seek God. Are you sincerely and faithfully seeking God?

The second condition that must be met if we want God to give us the desires of our heart is that we must we must personally answer the age old question, *"What then shall I do with Jesus who is called Christ?"* (Matt. 27:22). You see, when we seek God we *will* come face to face with Jesus. Jesus said, *"...I am the way, the truth, and the life. No one comes to the Father except through me"* (John 14:6). We must choose to follow Jesus Christ, to be His disciple. In Luke 9:23 Jesus said, *"...'if anyone desires to come after Me, let him deny himself, and take up his cross daily, and follow Me.'"* This second condition is where most of us have problems and where most of us fail to meet God's conditions.

Jesus says that in order to follow Him we must do three things. First we must deny ourselves. We must be humble and holy, meek and lowly. We we must embrace the Beatitudes (Matt. 5:1-16). We must constantly resist and overcome the natural urges of our fallen sinful nature. These sinful urges show up in the form of: (1)   impulses and desires for physical pleasure; (2) selfish and prideful mental thoughts patterns and opinions; and (3) emotional instability. We can overcome all of these effects of sin in our lives through prayer and praise, the word of God, and the power of God's Spirit.

THE FOOLISHNESS OF THE MESSAGE PREACHED

The second thing Jesus says we must do in order to follow Him is that we must pick up our cross daily. Must Jesus bear the cross alone, and all the world go free? No, we all must learn to live with conditions or situations that are not desirable to us. We all must put up with irritations in our lives. This is a method that God uses to shape us and mold us into the image and likeness of Christ. He prunes us that we may bear much fruit. While the process of being molded into the image of Christ may be uncomfortable to us, it is also very exciting because it is through this process that our dreams which have the most probability of coming true are born. You see, as we become more faithful and obedient to God, we begin to see things in a new light. Our value system is corrected and our lifestyle changes. We begin to realize that most of the dreams and desires that we use to have were foolish, immature, and superficial. The old dreams that we had which were planted in the soil of unfulfilled needs and selfish desires are uprooted and new dreams are born that will glorify God and conform to the will of God.

The third thing Jesus said we must do to follow him is follow Him. In other words, after we deny ourselves, pick up our cross, we must *follow* him. We must put into action what we believe and say. Jesus is saying, lights, camera, ACTION! Stop talking, start walking. In other words, just DO IT! We need to spend time reading God's word, studying God's word, meditating on God's Word, praying to God, praising God, loving one another, forgiving one another, encouraging one another, and living in faith and obedience by the power of His Spirit. Jesus said, "...*If you abide in My word, you are My disciple indeed*" (John 8:31). "*If you abide in Me, and My word abides in you,...it shall be done for you*" (John 15:7). We have to live this faith. Talk is cheap. If you have never accepted Jesus as your Lord and Savior, stop thinking about it and just do it.

Stop talking about what you need to do to live a life pleasing to God and just do it. If we want God to give us the desires of our heart, we must meet His conditions. First, we must seek God. Second, we must follow Christ. To follow Christ means we must: (1) deny ourselves; (2) pick up our cross daily; and, (3) follow Him.

The third condition I have discovered that must be met if we want God to give us the desires of our heart is we must ask for what we want. The word of God says, "*If you abide in Me and My words abide in you, you will ask what you desire, and it shall be done for you*" (John 15:7). Ask! James 4:2 says, "*...you have not because you ask not.*" Jesus said, "*...Ask, and you will receive, that your joy may be full*" (John 16:24). The third condition that we must meet if we want God to give us the desires of our hearts is that we must ask Him. We generally don't have a problem with asking.

What God is saying is that in order to increase the probability of our dreams coming true, we must strive to meet certain conditions. We must live a certain way, we must have a lifestyle that glorifies God. Even in the fairy tale story of Pinocchio, Geppetto had to live a certain way in order for His dream to come true. The granting of his dream come true was based on the fact that Geppetto had a certain lifestyle. Even Pinocchio had to live a certain way in order to have his dream come true. The granting of Pinocchio's dream come true was predicated on the fact that he had to live a certain lifestyle. If Geppetto and Pinocchio had to live a certain way in order for their dreams to come true, why is it that we Christians believe we can live any old kind of way and expect God to make our dreams come true? It doesn't even happen that way in fairy tales. Many of us fail to have our dreams and desires come true because we have not met God's conditions. We are not living our lives in a way that glorifies God and consequently we have not put ourselves in a position to claim what God has promised. We have to change our lifestyle.

When you meet these three conditions as set forth in the word of God, I have good news for you. God is still in the business of making dreams come true. When the desire of your heart is built on nothing less than Jesus' blood and His righteousness, don't be surprised if the dream you dream comes to you. Turn to your neighbor and say, "Neighbor, your dream is on its way." When you wish upon the Bright and Morning Star, called the Christ, dreams do come true. The Lord moves in mysterious ways, His wonders to perform.

Conclusion

This day I encourage you to dream once again. Strive to live a life that pleases God so that God's promise to make your dreams and desires come true can happen to you. God's promise is conditional. We must meet at least three conditions. We must: (1) Seek God; (2) Follow Jesus; and, (3) Ask God for what we want.

Stand on the promises of God that can not fail. Build your hope on things eternal. God's word is true. The devil is a liar. God will honor His word. Has your dream been deferred? Have you lost your ability to imagine a better tomorrow? Have you lost hope? Seek and you will find that in the kingdom of God, when you wish upon Christ, the Bright and Morning Star, dreams do come true. Thank you Walt Disney for reminding us that dreams do come true. Amen.

> I want to go, to that distant land (x3)
> Take my hand and lead me on....

> Come on, Come on, Come on, Don't you want to go (x3)
> Yes I want to Go....

Chapter 4

Living in a Dry and Thirsty Land

Scripture: Psalms 63:1; Revelation 17:22

Song: 1. *Even Me* (Elizabeth Codner)

Main Idea: Living apart from God is like living in a dry
and thirsty land.

> LORD, I hear of showers of blessings,
>   Thou art scattering full and free;
>   Showers, the thirsty land refreshing;
>   Let some droppings fall on me.
>   Even me.
>   *Even Me* (Elizabeth Codner)

Prolegomena

Isaiah, one of God's prophets said, "*The grass withers, the
flower fades, But the word of our God stands forever*" (Is.
40:8). Jesus said, "*Heaven and earth will pass away, but
My words will by no means pass away*" (Matt. 24:35). The
word of God is eternally important and when it comes to
preaching there are two questions that must be considered:
"What sayest the Scripture?" and "What sayest the Lord?"
If you would turn with me to Psalms 63:1; and, Revelation
17:22, we will read what sayest the Scripture. Reading from

the New King James Version, our primary scripture, Psalms 63:1, reads as follows:

> *O God, You are my God;*
> *Early will I seek You;*
> *My soul thirsts for You;*
> *My flesh longs for You*
> *In a dry and thirsty land*
> *Where there is no water.*
> [Ps 63:1]

Now turn to Revelation. As a complement to our primary text, Revelation 22:17 reads as follows,

> *And the Spirit and the bride say, "Come!"*
> *And let him who hears say, "Come!" And let*
> *him who thirsts come. And whoever desires,*
> *let him take the water of life freely.*
> [Rev. 17:22]

The title of this sermon is, "Living in a Dry and Thirsty Land."
     Pray.

Sermon Body

The phrase "a dry and thirsty land" is used in Psalms 63:1 to create in our minds a mental picture, a picture that will help us to understand God's message. When one thinks of a dry and thirsty land, what readily comes to mind is a desert, for a desert is a dry, desolate, barren, thirsty land. To the extent we can understand what living in a desert is like, we will better be able to grasp and understand what God is saying to us as He paints this picture on the canvas of our minds.

Approximately 70% of our planet's surface is water (Engel, 9). However, it is estimated that one-seventh (14%) of the land mass receives less than ten inches of rain per year (Leopold, 10). Such places are known as deserts. We need water to survive. Did you know that the total amount of water in a man of average weight is approximately 57% of his total body weight and in a newborn infant, this may be as high as 75% of the body weight (Guyton 1981, 391). Without water, we would look like California sun dried raisins. Well, since some of us are bigger than others, some of us would look more like prunes. If you don't want to go around looking like a raisin or prune, do not deprive yourself of water.

Living in the desert is risky. Although there are people who have learned to live by the rules of this dry land and have adapted to its harsh lifestyle and environment, it is generally recognized that even they are not exempt from nature's demands. So tenuous and dangerous is the life in the desert that even though the flora and the fauna labor desperately to survive, often, they succumb to the harsh elements and die. Living in a dry and thirsty land is dangerous. Most people would soon perish if they placed in the desert and deprived of a handy source of water and shelter from the sun. Living in a dry and thirsty land with little or no water is hazardous to your health (Ex. If your car has ever broke down on your way to from Los Angeles to Palm Springs or Las Vegas, then you understand what I'm talking about. Oh, come on, I know some of you church folk ride to Las Vegas almost every weekend in air conditioned cars and on luxury coaches but let something happen to that car, like a flat tire, or let that bus break down. After a few minutes in triple digit weather, I guarantee that you'll have a new attitude). I say, living in a dry and thirsty land is dangerous. I said it once and I'll say it again, living in a dry and thirsty land is dangerous.

One of the strangest things about some deserts is a hidden secret. The capacity of turning the dry, barren, wilderness into green pastures just lay a few feet below the hot, shifting sands. In May 1966, an article appeared in the journal *Scientific American* which revealed this truth (Ambroggi 1966, 21-29).

Robert Ambroggi wrote:

> The Sahara...possesses in abundance the remedy for aridity. Below the desert sands in water-bearing rock formations (aquifers) are huge quantities of water to sustain human settlement, pasturage for livestock and, in many places now barren, productive agriculture (Ambroggi 1966, 21-29).

You see, the problem in the desert is not infertility. When a freak rain storm occurs, the land blossoms and becomes fertile. He went on to point out that the entire Sahara desert contains no less than seven separate and distinct subterranean water systems that lie in wait to be used by whosoever shall cause the desert to bloom. Tragically, he wrote:

> There are no technological barriers to the prospect that the Sahara in many places and over large areas may now be made to bloom. The problems to be resolved in exploiting its huge resources of water are mainly political (Ambroggi 1966, 21-29).

In many ways, living in the desert is like living apart from God. To put it another way, living outside the will of God is like living in a dry and thirsty land. Listen very carefully. Living in the desert, with little or no water, can be likened to living your life with little or no fellowship with God. Let me repeat that. **Living in the desert, with little or no water, can be likened to living your life with little or no fellowship with God.** Watch this. If you attempt to live in the desert with little water, you have little chance of survival. If you attempt to live in the desert with no water, you have no chance of survival. If you attempt to live in the desert with much water, you have much chance of survival. Watch it now. Living in this phase of the end times consist of much spiritual warfare and we need much spiritual power to survive the attacks of the evil one. If we have little prayer with God, we have little power, if we have no prayer with God, we have no power. If we have much prayer with God, we have much spiritual power to survive the attacks of the devil.

If we spend little time reading and studying God's word, we have little power to build a firm foundation of hope amiss the shifting sands of these changing times. If we spend no time reading God's word, we have no power. If we spend much time studying God's word, we have much power to build our hopes on things eternal and hold to God's unchanging hand.

If we spend little time in the assembly of the household of faith, we have little power to access the supernatural support system God created within the church, if we spend no time going to church, we have no power. If we spend much time going to church, we have much power to obtain help from God through the individual and collective ministries that comprise the body of Christ. You see God has equipped every Christian with a spiritual gift or gifts for the work of ministry in the body of Christ. Whatever you need, God has someone in the church body that is equipped to meet your need, to help build you up, to make you strong, to equip you for the work of ministry (Eph. 4:11-12). Jesus designed the church to function in this manner.

Not only is living in a desert dangerous, living in a desert with little or no water will cause one to see things that are not there, especially when the heat goes up. You may see an oasis but learn that what you thought you saw was only a mirage. The same is true spiritually. When you are living outside the will of God, your sense of reality is altered, especially when the heat in the fiery furnace of trials and tribulations gets turned up. God tells us to walk by faith, not by sight (2 Cor. 5:7). If you live your life based on what you see you may not realize that what you see is a delusion, a mirage. The grass may look greener on the other side, but "It ain't necessarily so."

Living in a desert with little or nor water is dangerous. Living in a dry and thirsty land will make you see things that are not there. Living in a dry and thirsty land is like living with no thirst quenching, life sustaining power from the Lord. Are you living in a dry and thirsty land?

If you have not asked the Lord to come into your life as your personal Savior, guess what? You are living in a dry and thirsty land. You are attempting to live without water. Your chance for survival is zero. You will turn into a raisin.

If you have asked Jesus to be your personal savior but you are presently out of the ark of safety, that is, you do not belong to a local church body, guess what? You are living in a dry and thirsty land. God tells us do not forsake to assemble of ourselves together in Hebrews 10:25. You are living outside of the will of God! If you don't have a church home, GET ONE!

Maybe you attend a local church and your name is on the church role. But I tell you this, if you are in a church but the church is not in you, guess what? You are living in a dry and thirsty land. Believe it or not, from pulpit to pew, you can find prunes in the house of prayer.

If you preach and/or teach about being Christ-like but you don't act Christ-like, some people may say you are a hypocrite, living a lie, or perpetrating a fraud. Take what other people say with a grain of salt, they don't know the whole story. But take what God says to heart. God says that your are living in a dry and thirsty land. It's time to straighten up and fly right!

If you have not asked God to forgive you for the sins that you have committed this very day, guess what? You are living in a dry and thirsty land. I willing to bet you my bottom dollar that you have done some things God told you not to do and you have not done all that God has asked you to do. The Bible says, *"for all have sinned and fall short of the glory of Go*d" (Rom. 3:23) and that the penalty of sin is eternal death (Rom. 6:23). It says we are brought forth in iniquity and conceived in sin (Ps. 51:5). It says there is none who does good, *No, Not One* (Ps. 14:3). We need to repent and confess our sins to God daily and we need Jesus to get to God (John 14:6). We all, including me, are living in a dry and thirsty land because we all sin and sin separates us from God.

Not only do we all sin but we all are living in the end times. If you haven't noticed, today's society is becoming more and more ungodly and anti-Christian. According to a recent congressional report, there is abundant evidence of worldwide Christian persecution. We are living in a land where mothers sacrifice their unborn babies and small children to the ancient Babylonian god who now goes by the name of Convenience. We are living in a land where, instead of adults putting fear in their children, children put fear in adults. We are living in times where corruption rules the land, where few ministers have the courage to preach an uncompromising Gospel, where love seems to have gone on a holiday, where mercy seems to have lost her way. We are living in a land where people are bowing down to idols, fornicating with false religions, and committing mass suicides as part of cult rituals. We are living in times where freaky, deviant sexual behavior has become as common as toilet tissue. Homosexuality has become embraced socially, politically, and even has gained acceptance in some religious institutions. Its being promoted as an alternative, morally acceptable lifestyle, but to God it is, it was, and it always shall be an abomination and perversion (Lev. 18:22). We are living in a land that has broken fellowship with God. I tell you we are living in a dry and thirsty land.

If you realize that you are living in a dry and thirsty land, I want to tell you about a friend of mine who has the power to quench your thirst. Hallelujah! I have good news! I know somebody who has the power you need to survive in this dry and thirsty land! He died for your sins, He looked at death and said, O Death, where is your sting, O Hades, where is your victory (1 Cor. 15:55)? And He rose from the dead with all power in His hand! Say, "All Power."

> 1. I am so glad, Christ died for me;
>   way back on, Mt. Cal - var - y.
>   They stretched Him wide, and hung Him high;
>   blood came stream, 'n down His side.
>
> 2. My Jes - us cried, out with a voice;
>   bowed His head, by His own choice.
>   There was dark - ness, ov-er the land;
>   when He died, for sin - ful man.
>
> 3. He died with a, thorn crown they made;
>   death the price, for sin He paid.

The stain of sin, His blood did clean;
whit - er than, ev-er been seen.

4. And all the world, did fear His doom;
   when they sealed, Him in the tomb.
   They laid Him there, and there He stayed;
   in the tomb, no noise was made.

5. But ve-ry ear - ly third day morn;
   He be-came, my strong tow-er.
   Yes ear-ly ear-ly, Sun - day morn;
   JE-SUS ROSE, WITH ALL POW - ER!

6. Power, Power, Power, Power;
   All Power, Power, Power!
   Power, Power, Power, Power!
   All Power, Power, Power!
   (© 1997 Leonidas A. Johnson)

I talking about living in a dry and thirsty land.

Trying to survive the trials and tribulations of life when your relationship with God is broken by unconfessed sins is as dangerous as living in the desert with little water or no water. Just as there is an abundant water supply just a few feet underneath the hot sands of the Sahara desert, there is a Fountain of Living Waters just a prayer away. Through prayer we have access to this Fountain of Living Waters. God wants us to confess our sins before Him, repent of our sins, and ask Jesus to be our personal Savior. The Lord is the good shepherd and He will make us lie down in green pastures, where we can be nourished and spiritually fed. He wants to lead us besides still waters, but we have to want it too. We must bow down before we can lie down. Pride must sink before we may drink.

THE FOOLISHNESS OF THE MESSAGE PREACHED

Conclusion

What God is saying to us through this Scripture is that living outside the will of God is like living in a dry and thirsty land with no water. God is making a comparison. You know what a comparison is, right? Its like saying God is like Coke-a-Cola, He's the real thing. Its like saying God is like Pepto Bismo, He cures the upset stomach. It like saying God is like Alka Seltzer, plop plop fizz fizz oh what a relief, He is. It's like saying, God is like Green Eggs and Ham, try Him you'll like Him. It's like saying God is like Kellogg's Frosted corn flakes, He's Great. It's like saying God is like 92.3 The BEAT (Los Angeles), He erases all color lines. It's like saying God is like Gator Aid, He quenches your thirst. What God is saying to us is that He is the quench of our thirst. Not only is He the quench but He is our only source of water in a dry and thirsty land, a land that has no water. If you understand the comparison God is making in Psalms 63:1, then you understand that our chances of survival without God is zero, zero, zero! So we need to step up to throne, bow down, confess our sins to God in the name of the Lord Jesus Christ, and then drink from the Fountain of Living Waters.

And the Spirit and the bride say, "Come!"
And let him who hears say, "Come!" And let
him who thirsts come. And whoever desires,
let him take the water of life freely.
[Rev. 17:22]

God Bless You!

74

LIVING IN A DRY AND THIRSTY LAND

LORD, I hear of showers of blessings,
   Thou art scattering full and free;
Showers, the thirsty land refreshing;
   Let some droppings fall on me.
      Even me.

2   Pass me not, O God, our Father!
        Sinful though my heart may be;
     Thou might'st curse me, but the rather
        Let Thy mercy light on me.
           Even me.

3   Pass me not, oh, gracious Savior,
        Let me live and cling to Thee;
     For I am longing for Thy favor;
        Whilst Thou'rt calling, oh call me.
           Even me.

5   Love of God, so pure and changeless;
        Blood of Christ, so rich, so free;
     Grace of God, so strong and boundless;
        Magnify it all in me.
           Even me.
              Even Me (Elizabeth Codner)

BIBLIOGRAPHY

Ambroggi, Robert P. "Water Under the Sahara," *Scientific American*, May 1966, pp. 21-29, quoted in Dr. Lubrett Hargrove, "The Gospel Truth: Dry Deserts, Bitter Waters, and the Second Coming," Bible In The News. July 1997, N-084, Oklahoma City: Southwest Radio Church.

Engel, Leonard. The Sea. New York: Time Inc., quoted in Dr. Lubrett Hargrove, "The Gospel Truth: Dry Deserts, Bitter Waters, and the Second Coming," Bible In The News. July 1997, N-084, Oklahoma City: Southwest Radio Church.

Guyton, Arthur, C. Textbook of Medical Physiology 6th ed. Philadelphia:W.B. Saunders Co., 1981.

Leopold, A. Starker. The Desert. New York: Time, Inc. quoted in Dr. Lubrett Hargrove, "The Gospel Truth: Dry Deserts, Bitter Waters, and the Second Coming," Bible In The News. July 1997, N-084, Oklahoma City: Southwest Radio Church.

REFERENCES

Batmanghelidj, M.D., F. 1997. Your Body's Many Cries ForWater: You Are Not Sick, You Are Thirsty! Don't Treat Thirst with Medications! Falls Church, Virginia: Global Health Solutions, Inc.

Chapter 5

Dr. Do Little, Please Do More

Text: Matt. 9:35-38; 10:1

Songs: 1. *Only What You Do for Christ Will Last*
          (Raymond Rasberry)
      2. *May the Work I've Done Speak for Me*
          (Sullivan Pugh)
      3. *God Hired Me* (Traditional)

Main Idea: There is a need for more Christian Ministry
            workers.

You may build great cathedrals large or small,
You can build sky scrapers grand and tall,
You may conquer all the failures of the past,
But only what you do for Christ will last.
Only What You Do for Christ Will Last
(Raymond Rasberry)

Prolegomena

All praises to God who is the head of my life, to the pastor
of this great church, pulpit ministers, officers, members,
visitors and special guests, it is indeed a privilege to stand

77

before you today as God's messenger. Please turn to Matthew 9:35. There you will find recorded:

> *And Jesus went about all the cities and villages, teaching in their synagogues, preaching the gospel of the kingdom, and healing every sickness and every disease among the people. But when He saw the multitudes, He was moved with compassion for them, because they were weary and scattered, like sheep having no shepherd. Then He said to His disciples, "The harvest truly is plentiful, but the laborers are few. Therefore pray the Lord of the harvest to send out laborers into His harvest." And when He had called His twelve disciples to Him, He gave them power over unclean spirits, to cast then out and to heal all kinds if sickness and all kinds of disease.*
> [Matt. 9:35-38; 10:1]

I would like to speak to you from the title, "Dr. Do Little please Do more."

Pray.

Introduction

As God prepared me to deliver this message, He reminded me of the story of the Little Red Hen. For those of you who are not familiar with this story, allow me a moment to familiarize you with this children's story.

It just so happened that one day a Little Red Hen was scratching in the farmyard, when she found a grain of wheat. "Who will plant the wheat?" asked the Little Red

Hen. The wise old owl said "Who?" "Not I," said the cat. "Not I," said the pig. "Not I," said the goat. "Very well then," said the Little Red Hen, "I will." So she planted the grain of wheat.

"Who will water the wheat?" asked the Little Red Hen. The wise old owl said "Who?" "Not I," said the cat. "Not I," said the pig. "Not I," said the goat. "Very well then," said the Little Red Hen, "I will." So she water the wheat faithfully.

After some time the wheat grew tall and ripe. "Who will cut the wheat?" asked the Little Red Hen. The wise old owl said "Who?" "Not I," said the cat. "Not I," said the pig. "Not I," said the goat. "Very well then," said the Little Red Hen, "I will." So she cut the wheat.

"Now," she said, "who will thresh the wheat?" The wise old owl said "Who?" "Not I," said the cat. "Not I," said the pig. "Not I," said the goat. "Very well then," said the Little Red Hen, "I will." So she threshed the wheat.

When the wheat was threshed, she said, "Who will take the wheat to the mill to have it ground into flour?" The wise old owl said "Who?" "Not I," said the cat. "Not I," said the pig. "Not I," said the goat. "Very well then," said the Little Red Hen, "I will." So she took the wheat to the mill.

When the wheat was ground into flour, she said, "Who will make this flour into bread?" The wise old owl said "Who?" "Not I," said the cat. "Not I," said the pig. "Not I," said the goat. "Very well then," said the Little Red Hen, "I will." So she baked a lovely loaf of bread.

Then she said, "Who will eat the bread?" "Oh! I will," said the owl. "Oh! I will," said the cat. "Oh! I will," said the pig. "Oh! I will," said the goat. "Oh, no, you won't!" said the Little Red Hen.

You are probably wondering what this story has to do with you. The story of the Little Red Hen will help to illustrate three biblical principles involving the work of Christian ministry.

Sermon Body

The first principle I should like to bring to your attention regarding the work of Christian ministry is that the work of Christian ministry involves physical effort. The scripture says that, "...*Jesus went about all the cities and villages, teaching in their synagogues, preaching the gospel of the kingdom, and healing every sickness and every disease among the people*" (Matt. 9:35). You must remember, unlike today, in biblical times there were no airplanes, no trains, no buses, and no cars. No, there were no bicycles. There were no five-star, five-diamond, air-conditioned, luxury resorts and fine hotels for Jesus to stay in. Jesus was financially poor. You may recall He had to borrow a donkey to ride into Jerusalem on what we celebrate as Palm Sunday. Contrary to popular opinion, Jesus taught by example that the work of Christian ministry involves physical effort.

Now days we are reluctant to make physical effort to do Christian ministry. Now days we don't want to *go* walk, to *go* help the needy. Now days we don't want to *go* catch the bus, to *go* visit with our brothers and sisters who are grieving the lost of a love one. Now days we don't want to *go* catch the train, to *go* visit the sick and shut-in. Now days, we don't want to *go* use our car, to *go* deliver food and clothing to the needy. Now days, we don't want to *go* ahead and use some initiative and put forth some effort to *go* to school, *go* fill out a job application, etc. to help our own self let alone *go* across town to help some widows, orphans, and children in need of our support. Now days, we don't even want to put forth the physical effort to *go* get

80

that old bicycle out the garage to give it to someone in need of transportation. All this in the presence of Jesus' command to **GO** unto all the nations (Matt. 28:19). My, my, my.

If the church is to feed and clothe the homeless, somebody has to bring food and clothing to the church. Who? Somebody has to organize and stock the materials. Who? Somebody has to deliver and distribute the materials. Who? "Who? Me? Do that? Not I said the cat!"

My brothers and sister, when there is a need for something to be done that involves physical effort, somebody must put forth some physical effort to fulfill that unmet need. When the Little Red Hen needed certain jobs to be done that involved physical effort, someone had to do some work. Someone had to plant the wheat, someone had to water the wheat, someone had to cut the wheat, someone had to thresh the wheat, someone had to take to wheat to the mill, someone had to bake the bread. The work of Christian ministry involves physical effort. Unmet emotional and spiritual needs often involve some form of physical effort in the process of fulfilling those needs. It's all right to pray but sometimes, its takes more than that. Don't just tell me you love me, show me. Don't just talk about faith in Christ, show me your faith by your works. Don't just sing about hope, live it. Don't just pray for me, roll up your shelves and help me.

The work of Christian ministry involves more than just sitting in the pew. We have too many people in our churches who do little. Too many *Do Littles* is not good. *Do Little* people like to congregate in large local churches because they can hide from duty. They come to church, sit on the pew and then go home. Often they come from smaller churches where they were very active but now they want to take a break from the work of Christian ministry so they find a large congregation and hide in the crowd.

Former Sunday school teachers, deacons, choir members, even some preachers might try to get away with it. Their new motto is, lay low and do as little as possible. To them, the new work ethic of Christian ministry may consist of staying home, watching T.V., maybe thinking about the what's going on at the church, and every now and then, saying a brief prayer. Contrary to popular belief, the work of Christian ministry does involve physical effort.

Not only does the work of Christian ministry involve physical effort, the work of Christian ministry involves more than one person. The Bible says,

> "But when He saw the multitudes, He was moved with compassion for them, because they were weary and scattered, like sheep having no shepherd. Then He said to His disciples, "The harvest is plentiful, but the laborers are few. Therefore pray the Lord of the harvest to send out into His harvest" [Matt. 9:36-38].

Jesus was a busy man, going from city to city, village to village, teaching, preaching, and healing the sick. That was a lot of work for one man. According to Matthew's arrangement of the gospel, Jesus was busy working, but when He saw the multitudes, Jesus realized that there was much more work to do than he alone could physically handle. Jesus was working under the same conditions that many of us are faced with in our ministry. The work of Christian ministry can seem overbearing at times. Sometime its seems as though we are carrying the whole load. Sometimes it seems as though God's program depends solely on us and we get these funny attitudes like the prophet Elijah. When he thought he was the only prophet left in Israel who had not forsaken the Lord God he fled. He stopped doing what God called and equipped him to do (1 Kings 19:14).

In the face of tremendous amounts of Christian ministry work Jesus, not only continued to work but, demonstrated a positive attitude. Even though there was more physical work than Jesus could humanly do, Jesus never seemed to complain because the heavy work load. He never is reported to have poked out his lips, pouted, stormed away in anger, or abandoned His duties because of all the work He had to do. Never in scripture is it recorded that Jesus said, "Who? Me? Do All That! No Way! You Must be joking!" In other words, there was never a "Not I, said the cat" situation with Jesus. No, we don't see Jesus complaining in scripture regarding doing the work of Christian ministry.

When we are busy working for Jesus Christ, even though it may seem as though we are the only ones carrying the load, we must keep on working with a positive attitude like Jesus. When Jesus was face with overwhelming workload, He pressed toward the mark. He wasn't concerned about what Tom, Dick, or Harry was or was not doing. He wasn't concerned about what Sally, Sue, or Mary Lou was saying. Instead, He remained focused on his task. He said , "*I must work the works of Him who sent me while it is day; the night is coming when no one can work*" (John 9:4). Jesus said, "*...My food is to do the will of Him who sent Me, and to finish His work*" (John 4:34). My, my, my! When faced with overwhelming work demands, we must stopping focusing on all the mess that going on around us and do our job of lifting up the name of Jesus. We must remain focused that our food is to do the will of God. Like Christ, we must press on with a positive attitude, striving to please God.

The Little Red Hen thought she was the only one working. While it is true that no one volunteered to help her plant, water, cut, or thresh the wheat. Even though no one volunteered to help her take the wheat to the mill or make the flour into bread, she did receive help. Even though it seemed as though she did everything by herself, she did have help. At the mill, someone else ground the wheat into flour. So it is in the work of Christian Ministry. Often times we feel as though we are doing everything but we must remember, the work of Christian ministry involves more than just one person. Elijah learned that he wasn't the only prophet left. Over in 1 Kings 19:18 the Bible tells us that God had a talk with Elijah. God told Elijah that there were seven thousand prophets in Israel that had not bowed to Baal, the idol god (1 Kings 19:18). When we are in the trenches of doing the work of Christian Ministry, we may feel as though we are the only ones but God wants you to know you are not the only one. Don't leave your post. Stay on the battlefield. Hold up the blood stain banner. Help is on the way. Jesus looked up and saw He needed help. The work of Christian Ministry involves more than just one person.

Not only does the work of Christian Ministry involve physical effort and not only does the work of Christian ministry involves more than just one person, the work of Christian Ministry involves you and me. Turn to your neighbor and repeat after me, God has called and equipped you for the work of Christian ministry. The Bible says, *"And when He had called His twelve disciples to Him, He gave them power over unclean spirits, to cast then out and to heal all kinds if sickness and all kinds of disease"* (Matt. 10:1). Alleluia! In Luke 10:19 Jesus says,

Behold, I give you the authority to trample on serpents and scorpions, and over all the power of the enemy, and nothing shall by any means hurt you. Nevertheless do not

84

*rejoice in this, that the spirits are subject to
you, but rather rejoice because your names
are written in heaven* [Luke 10:19].

Praise God! If you are a disciple of Jesus Christ, God has
not only called you but equipped you for the work of
Christian ministry! Are you a disciple? Are you a follower
of Christ? Jesus said, "*...If you abide in My word, you are
My disciple indeed*" (John 8:31).

If we have accepted Jesus Christ as our Lord and
Savior and as a result have received the gift of eternal life
by God's Grace through faith in Jesus Christ and have been
given at least one spiritual gift as ministers and
ambassadors for Christ and commissioned by our Lord to
go and make disciples of all the nations, why is it that when
we are asked to do something for Christ in the local
Church, the first thing that comes out of our mouths is,
"Who? Me?" Why is it that with our actions we say, "Not I,
said the cat!" I know that don't happen in this church, I'm
taking about them other Christians in them other churches.
I know you don't have a problem with getting people to
volunteer there time, money, and effort to help promote the
kingdom of God. I know you don't have a problem finding
committed Sunday school teachers who are willing to
prepare themselves to teach eager minds thirsty for the
Living Bread. You don't have officers who stay home to
watch sports. You don't have ministers and other church
leaders who show up once every blue moon, who shuck and
jive on their leadership responsibilities and commitments.
No, not at this church you don't have them kind of
problems. Choir members and ushers are always on duty
here. I know you have good attendance at all church
meetings. I'm sure you don't have any people here who go
around saying in action and deeds, "Not I, said the cat." As
when Isaiah heard the question posed, "Who will go for

85

us?" I'm sure all the people in this church gladly replied, "Here am I! Send me" (Isaiah 6:8).

Just in case there are some people here who are not so inclined to partake in the work of Christian ministry, allow me to extend you God's invitation. Anyone who is not giving God his or her best in service, please do more. Too many of us do too little to help our pastor, too little to help our young people grow up to fear God, which is the beginning of wisdom, too little to support church activities and ministries, too little to change ungodly laws, too little to defend the rights of the oppressed, too little to care for widow and orphans, too little to lift the Savior up. We need to stop doing as little as possible and do more. The church is filled with too many professional *Do Littles* in the face the opportunities to do more. Are you a professional *Do little*? God is saying to you, *Dr. Do Little*, please do more.

Generations before you have made tremendous sacrifices to afford you the opportunities and comforts of your present day lifestyle. Stop eating the fruits of other people's labor without putting forth effort to improve conditions for the next generation. It is ashamed to loose gains of the past. We have become lazy and complacent. We are easily distracted and have lost the concept of commitment. We are slipping in the darkness of mediocracy. Jesus said, "...*he who does not take his cross and follow after Me is not worthy of Me*" (Matt. 10:38). Jesus said,

> *Do you not say, 'There are still four months and then comes the harvest'? Behold, I say to you, lift up your eyes and look at the fields, for they are already white for harvest! And he who reaps receives wages, and gathers fruit for eternal life, that both he*

who sows and he who reaps may rejoice together [John 4:35-36].

Unlike the owl, the cat, the pig, and the goat who were not invited to eat the Little Red Hen's fresh loaf of bread because they were not willing to make a physical contribution to the work of making the bread, Christians who do make a contribution toward the work of Christian ministry gather fruit for eternal life and are invited to the marriage supper of the Lamb.

Conclusion

The work of Christian ministry involves physical effort. The work of Christian ministry involves more than just one person. The work of Christian ministry involves you and me. God has called and equipped us for the job. If you are doing little, God is asking you to adjust your priorities, adjust your schedules, and do more. It is important. Only what you do for Christ will last. If you are a professional do little, you do little Christian ministry work, God is asking you, starting today, to please do more. *Dr. Do Little*, please do more.
Amen.

God Hired Me, Sure do Like My Job (x3)
I do, I do, I do.

1. God hired me to preach, Sure do like my job.
2. God hired me to sing,...
3. God hired me to pray,...
4. God hired me to serve,...
God Hired Me (Traditional)

THE FOOLISHNESS OF THE MESSAGE PREACHED

Chapter 6

Where Is Your Hyde?

Text: 2 Corinthians 5:17

Songs: 1. *I've Got a New Name* (Traditional)
       2. *I know that I'm, a Child of God* (Old Meter)
       3. *Old Meter Hymn Spin-offs* (Traditional)

Main Idea: We have a new nature in Christ.

> I know that I'm, a Child of God
> That's why I move, so slow.
> *Old Meter Hymn*

> The Lord is my Shepherd
> I shall not want.
> Lord I'm down here waiting,
> Can't do nothing 'til you come.
> *Old Meter Hymn Spin-offs*

Prolegomena

All praises to God who is the head of my life, to the pastor of this great church, pulpit ministers, officers, members, visitors and special guests, it is indeed a privilege to stand before you today as God's messenger. Please turn with me to Romans 7:15-24. There it reads as follows:

For what I am doing, I do not understand. For what I will to do, that I do not practice; but what I hate, that I do. If, then, I do what I will not to do, I agree with the law that it is good. But now, it is no longer I who do it, but sin that dwells in me. For I know that in me (that is, in my flesh) nothing good dwells; for to will is present with me, but how to perform what is good I do not find. For the good I will to do, I do not do; but the evil I will not to do, that I practice. Now if I do what I will not to do, it is no longer I who do it but sin that dwells in me. I find then a law, that evil is present with me, the one who wills to do good. For I delight in the law of God according to the inward man. But I see another law in my members. O wretched man that I am! Who will deliver from this body of death? [Romans 7:15-24]

Now turn to 2 Corinthians 5:17. There you will find recorded:

Therefore if anyone is in Christ, he is a new creation; old things have passed away; behold, all things have become new.
[2 Corinthians 5:17]

Let me hear you say new. God's message to you today is entitled, *Where is Your Hyde?* By the end of this sermon, with God's help, you will be able to answer the question, *Where is Your Hyde?*
   Pray.

WHERE IS YOUR HYDE?

Introduction

There was a popular story written many years ago about a gentleman who went by the name Dr. Jekyll. Dr. Jekyll's story is not only a story about Dr. Jekyll but it is a story about you and me. You see, Dr. Jekyll had a problem that we all share in common and his story is our story. Though his story is fictional our story is real. Though his story was the product of someone's imagination, our story is the product of life experiences. Let us take a look at this story and see what spiritual truths God would have us gleam from it.

Sermon Body

The story of *Dr. Jekyll and Mr. Hyde* written by Robert Stevenson is interesting, to say the least. As the story goes, Dr. Jekyll was an upright but uptight gentleman. He was raised in Victorian England with a strict sense of good and evil. Dr. Jekyll was a good man. He was a mild mannered, well behaved gentleman. But Dr. Jekyll was tormented by evil impulses, which he sometimes secretly indulged. He heard voices that *urged* him to do naughty things. And, every now and then, he would tip toe out and misbehave. We do the same thing.

There are things that we know we shouldn't do and places we shouldn't go but every now we get the *urge* to secretly hang out in local places that are forbidden and the *urge* to do things we have no business doing. We get the *urge* to boldly go to far away places to avoid going around in cognitio and we get the *urge* to get our groove on. Lord have mercy. If God showed the film of how you acted on your last trip. Goodness gracious alive! In our anger we get the *urge* to maliciously attack and disrespect the

91

personhood and character of other people. The Bible says, "Be angry, and do not sin" (Ps. 4:4a). We get the *urge* to dismiss and/or distort God's design for civil law and order. But why did you shoot the man? "I don't know." We get the *urge* to be morally irresponsible and to rebel against Gods moral laws. We get the *urge* to be unfaithful. Adultery and fornication are still reigning leaders of moral decay. We get the *urge* to almost get caught, "That was exciting we almost got caught, let's do it again!" We get the *urge* to lie and cheat our way through life. We like the idea of getting something for nothing, especially if it means mo' money in our pocket. So, we must fight the *urge* to break the law, to violate rules and regulations to get gain without pain. These and other *urges* we experience have satanic origins, demonic dimensions, and how we deal with them have eternal repercussions.

Dr. Jekyll's problem, and indeed, our problem is that we experience the *urge* to do evil in the site of a Holy and Righteous God. Dr. Jekyll was not happy being good nor was he happy being bad. When his behavior was good, evil impulses tormented him and when his behavior was bad his active conscience plagued him with guilt. Dr. Jekyll was miserable. "Should I or shouldn't I?" can be a difficult question to answer sometimes! Anybody know what I'm taking about?

As the story goes, Dr. Jekyll tried a chemical solution to his dilemma. Dr. Jekyll thought by drinking a certain potion that he could solve his problem. He thought that the solution was to separate his good and his evil nature. He theorized,

> If each, I told myself, could be housed in
> separate identities, life would be relieved of
> all that was unbearable; the unjust might go
> his way, delivered from the aspirations and

remorse of his more upright twin; and the just could walk steadfastly and securely on his upward path...no longer exposed to the disgrace and penitence by the hands of this extraneous evil (Stevenson, 1964).

Dr. Jekyll is like many of us. Many of us have tried a chemical solution to the dilemmas and problems we've confronted in life. Am I right? We have tried alcohol. We have tried tobacco. We have tried prescription drugs like Prozac, Valium, and even Tylenol with Codeine. We have tried illegal drugs like marijuana, crack, cocaine, PCP, methamphetamines, etc. Chemical solutions to problems don't always work. In fact, many times they make things worse and confuse the issues. Have you been looking for a chemical solution to solve your dilemma. Have you been trying to smoke and/or drink your problem away? Are you being victimized by the demons of substance abuse? Dr. Jekyll thought he discovered a solution to his problem. Dr. Jekyll thought he could solve his problem with a chemical substance. Dr. Jekyll was wrong!

Dr. Jekyll didn't realize that instead of making things better he made things worse. As a result of using this chemical, Dr. Jekyll ended up with the dissociative disorder known as MPD, Multiple Personality Disorder, a condition in which there are distinct and separate personalities within the same person, each of which when present dominates the person's attitudes, behavior, and selfview, as though no other personality exists" (Kaplin 1990, 119). Dr. Jekyll successfully created two distinct personalities, a good Dr. Jekyll and a bad Mr. Hyde, but He lost control of who he was and who was in charge. Dr. Jekyll would dissociate and the evil Mr. Hyde would suddenly and uncontrollable surface at the most inopportune times and take control over Dr. Jekyll. Putting the chemical into his body caused him to develop mental illness. Putting drugs in your body can cause mental illness. I say when you put certain chemicals into your body you invite demons into your life and you end up making things worse. Let me hear you say worse. Dr. Jekyll's experiment was a failure.

Dr. Jekyll's attempt to deal with the tug-of-war battle between good and evil on the battlefield of his mind is our story. This is our story. This is our song. Trying to find a solution to this moral madness all the day long. If you think you can solve your problems with chemical substances like Dr. Jekyll, you are dead wrong. You are traveling down the wrong path, a path that may lead to mental illness and eternal darkness. We must walk in the Light. We must walk where the dew drops of God's mercy shines bright. Then we can discover how to successfully deal with the problem of evil impulses taking control over our lives.

In our scripture the Apostle Paul sheds some light on this age old problem described in the story of *Dr. Jekyll and Mr. Hyde.* Paul, was like many of us. Paul loved the Lord and wanted to please God. Many of us love the Lord and want to please God. However, Paul discovered that even when he desired to do the things that were pleasing to God, evil was always present. In fact, when he desired to do good, he did the opposite.

For example, Paul knew it was godly to love everybody, but he discovered that there were some people he just simple didn't like. Like Paul, there are people we just don't like. There are people we won't speak to. There are people we just don't want to see or deal with at times. It may be your boss. It may be a co-worker. It may be your spouse. It may be people right here in this church. Paul had a problem getting along with some church folk too. Oh yeah! Didn't you know church folk have fought with church folk since the first century when the local church was first instituted. Yes, even the Apostle Paul, this great statue and pillar of faith, this outstanding writer and missionary of the early church, this great preacher who urged Euodia and Synthtyche to be of the same mind in the Lord recorded in Philippians 4:2, this Apostle himself had a major disagreement with a fellow coworker in the cause of Christ. Barnabas wanted to take John Mark on Paul's second missionary journey, Paul disagreed. The disagreement got so heated that and they ended up spiting and going opposite ways. Barnabas took Mark and when one way, Paul took Silas and went another. Check it out in Acts 15:36-40. Church folks fighting each other. Church folks not speaking to each other. Church folks scandalizing and destroying the reputations of other church folk. It happened to people in the Bible and it is happens to us. Well, preacher, how do we deal with these evil impulses that torment us and tempt us to say and do the opposite of what thus says the Lord? That's a good question. Let's deal with it.

The Real Problem

Dr. Jekyll's uncontrolled evil urges resulted from his sin nature and he tried to fix the sin problem without changing his sin nature. Our problem is our sin nature. The Bible says all humans are born with an innate tendency to rebel against God and reject God's love. The first step in solving the problem of the tug-of-war problem between the good and evil in us is to change our sin nature.

How do we change the sin nature? That 's a good question. The answer is, we can't. If the problem is in our sin nature, and if we are not able to change our sin nature, who, then, is able?

The Only Solution

There is only one way to change our sin nature. The Bible states that when we accept Jesus Christ in faith as our personal Savior, by the grace of God, this miraculous change takes place. God is **able** to change our sin nature. Check out the scripture in 2 Corinthians 5:17:

> *Therefore if anyone is in Christ, he is a new creation; old things have passed away; behold, all things have become new.*
> [2 Corinthians 5:17]

When you accept Christ by faith you become a new creation. Let me hear you say, "NEW." Your nature is instantly and permanently changed.

Because of your new nature that results from this new creation, this positional change, this transformation, this metamorphosis, **GOD DECLARES** that you are:

The salt of the earth (Matt.5:13), *the light of the world* (Matt. 5:14), *a child of God* (John 1:12; Rom. 8:14,15; Gal. 3:26; 4:6), *a part of the True Vine, a branch of Jesus Christ* (John 15:1,5), *chosen and appointed by Jesus Christ to bear His fruit* (John 15:16), *a joint heir with Jesus Christ, sharing His inheritance with Him* (Rom. 8:17), *a temple, a dwelling place of the Spirit of God* (1 Cor. 3:16; 6:19), *united to the Lord* (1 Cor. 6:17), *a member of Christ's body* (1 Cor. 12:27; Eph. 5:30), *reconciled to God and a minister of reconciliation* (2 Cor. 5:18,19), *God's workmanship* (Eph. 2:10), *a fellow citizen with the family of God* (Eph. 2:19), *a citizen of heaven* (Phil. 3:20; Eph. 2:6) *chosen of God, holy and dearly loved* (Col. 3:1; 1 Thess. 1:4), *a child of the light and not of the darkness* (1 Thess. 5:5), *a partaker of a heavenly calling* (Heb. 3:1), *one of God's living stones, being built up in Jesus Christ as a spiritual house* (1 Pet. 2:5), *a member of a chosen race, a royal priesthood, a holy nation, a people for God's own possession* (1 Pet. 2:9,10), *an alien and stranger to this world in which we temporarily live* (1 Pet. 2:11), *an ambassador for Jesus Christ* (2 Cor. 5:20), *an enemy of the devil* (1 Pet. 5:8), *righteous and holy* (Eph. 4:24; 2 Cor. 5:21), *a saint* (Eph 1:1; 1 Cor 1:2; Phil. 1:1; Col 1:2)!

The first step in dealing with this tug-of-war sin problem is to change our sin nature. We are unable to do this, but God is. God is ready, willing, and able!

The second step in dealing with this sin problem is to accept our new identity in Christ. Let me hear you say, "NEW." As a born again Christian you are not the same person you use to be so you need to stop thinking of yourself in the same way! Born again Christians are not sinners, we are saints! Our behavior may not be saintly but we are, none the less saints, identified with Christ. Why do you think of yourself as a sinner when God has declared you righteous? Even though it may be correct in one sense to say that we are sinners saved by the grace of God, that message has been distorted by the devil and is being used to keep many Christian stuck in a mental cocoon of old thinking.

THE FOOLISHNESS OF THE MESSAGE PREACHED

The devil knows that no person can consistently live in a manner that is different and inconsistent with how that person views or perceives him/herself (Anderson, 1990, p.50). If you think like an ugly duck, you will act like an ugly duck and quack like a ugly duck, though you may be a beautiful swan. If you think you are a chicken, you will act like a chicken, though you may be an eagle. If you think you are inferior, you will accept being treated as though you were inferior, though you may be equal. If you think you are in bondage you will act as though you are in bondage, though you may be free. Let me hear you say, "FREE."

We need to renew our minds so that our thinking is consistent with our new nature, our new identity in Christ. The Bible says,

> *that you put off, concerning your former conduct, the old man which grows corrupt according to the deceitful lusts, and be renewed in the spirit of your mind, and that you put on the new man which was created according to God, in righteousness and true holiness.* [Eph. 4:23,24; cf Rom. 12:1-2]

The Bible says that when you accept Christ as your personal savior, your nature is changed. Let me hear you say, "CHANGED." The first step in dealing with this sin problem is to change our sin nature. God does this for us. The second step in dealing with this sin problem is to change our attitude. We must do this step, we need to accept our new identity in Christ.

The third step in dealing with this sin problem is to change our habits. We must study the Bible (2 Tim. 2:15). We need to strengthen our new nature by drinking the sincere milk of God's word (1 Pet. 2:1-3). The Bible says that,

> *All Scripture is given by inspiration of God, and is profitable for doctrine, for reproof, for correction, for instruction in righteousness, that the man of God may be complete, thoroughly equipped for every good work.* [2 Tim. 3:16-17]

All habits and other aspects of your behavior may not change instantaneously the day you accept Jesus as your personal Lord and Savior. Though the behavior of the sinner and the saint may look similar, there is an important difference between the two. The sinner sins because the sinner is powerless to overcome sin and will eventually die. The sinner needs deliverance. A saint sins as part of a process of spiritual growth and maturation. The saint has been delivered from the power of sin and will eventually experience victory over all sin and death. Positionally our sanctification is instantaneous the moment we accept Christ but experientially some of our behavior may not reflect our new nature, it takes time. There is a process of growth and maturation, a series of steps and changes God guides us through as we approach ultimate sanctification in heaven with our glorified resurrection bodies. In the mean time God has given us His word as a weapon and His Spirit not only as a source of power but also as a guarantee of our ultimate victory over all evil.

Conclusion

Where is your Hyde? My Hyde died when I accepted King Jesus as my Lord and Savior. I accept my new identity in

THE FOOLISHNESS OF THE MESSAGE PREACHED

Christ and I strive to study the word of God to show myself approve unto God, rightly diving the word of truth. Look at me. I may not be what I want to be or what you think I ought to be but by the grace of God I am not what I use to be. Be patient with me. God is not through with me yet. When God gets through with me, I shall come forth as pure gold. Take another look at me. I AM CHANGING! The road is rough the going gets though the hills are hard to climb. I've decided to make Jesus my choice and I'm going to make it. If your Hyde has not died, then the first step is to change your sin nature. Accept Jesus as your personal Savior today, don't delay. Secondly, change your attitude. Accept your new identity in Christ. Thirdly, change your habits. Study God's word. I invite you to come today.
        Amen.

BIBLIOGRAPHY

Kaplan,M.D, Harold I. and Benjamin J. Sadock, M.D.
        Pocket Handbook of Clinical Psychiatry
        Baltimore:Williams & Wilkins, 1990.

Stevenson, Robert Louis, Dr. Jekyll and Mr. Hyde. New
        York: Arco Publishing Company, 1964, 78.
        Quoted in Stephen H. Shoemaker. The Jekyll &
        Hyde Syndrome, 11-12, Nashville: Broadman
        Press, 1987.

REFERENCES

Anderson, Neil T. 1990. Victory over the Darkness:
        Realizing the Power of Your Identity in Christ
        Ventura: Regal Books.

Chapter 7

The Greatest Wizard of All

Text: Eph. 6:10-12; 2 Cor.10:3-5

Background: 2 Cor. 11:3,14; 2 Cor. 2:11-13;
              1 Pet. 5:8; Rev. 12:9; 1 John 3:8;

Songs: 1. *The Lord Will Make a Way Somehow*
          (Thomas A. Dorsey)
       2. *Move Up A Little Higher* (Annie Haley)

Main Idea: Satan is a Defeated Deceiver.

Prolegomena

To the pastor of this great church, pulpit ministers, officers, members, and visitors, it is a great honor and privilege for me to stand before you to proclaim this liberating, soul saving message from my Heavenly Father. By the authority that God has been given me I command the devil and the powers of darkness to release from captivity those that accept in faith this message preached, in the name of Jesus.
   Please turn with me to Ephesians 6:10-12:

> *Finally, my brethren, be strong in the Lord and in the power of His might. Put on the whole armor of God, that you may be able to stand against the wiles of the devil. For we*

> *do not wrestle against flesh and blood, but against principalities, against powers, against rulers of the darkness of this age, against spiritual hosts of wickedness in the heavenly places.* [Eph. 6:10-12]

Also turn to 2 Cor. 10:3-5. There it reads:

> *For though we walk in the flesh, we do not war according to the flesh. For the weapons of our warfare are not carnal but mighty in God for pulling down strongholds, casting down arguments and every high thing that exalts itself against the knowledge of God, bringing every thought into captivity to the obedience of Christ.* [2 Cor. 10:3-5]

The title of today's sermon is, **The Greatest Wizard of All**.

Pray.

Sermon Body

The Wizard of Oz is a story about a girl named Dorothy who encountered a terrible storm in the youth of her life. During the storm she was stuck in the head. When she regained consciousness from this blow to the head she discovered that she was in the strange land of OZ, a land of small people, little munchkins. A land where the people lived in fear of witches and wizards. The Wizard of Oz is the story of Dorothy's journey home. She is instructed by these little people to follow the yellow brick road to the Emerald City and seek out the great Wizard of Oz who is able to do great and marvelous things. On her journey to the Emerald City in the land of Oz she meets a scarecrow with no sense, a tin man with no heart, and a lion with no courage.

Many of us have encountered various storms in life. The storms I'm referring to are not storms resulting from atmospheric turbulence but storm clouds of adversity resulting from personal (Eph. 6:10-13, 2 Cor 12, 1 Pet. 5:8), institutional (Rev. 2:13), and territorial (Dan 10; 2 Kings 6:15-19) warfare waged in heavenly places. These storms of life have a way of knocking us to our knees. These storms may even cause us to wonder, "Where is God when I need Him?" During these storms we are subject to be hit up side the head with all kinds of terrible emotional and psychological blows. You were sexually violated. You're spouse wants a divorce after 20 years of marriage. You're HIV positive. You have cancer. Your child was struck by a stray bullet as a result of random violence. Dorothy was caught in a storm and was physically knocked senseless. We are often caught in storms and emotionally and psychologically are knocked senseless.

Dorothy emerged from her blow in the head in a strange world. Have you known anyone who, after going through a serious issue in life, now walk around with a strange new distorted perspective on life? Dorothy was like a giant in a land of small people. We sometimes walk around as though we are giants in a land of small people. We ignore and dismiss the concerns of other people as small and insignificant. Ever since old Charlie's wife died he "ain't" been the same. Ever sine the doctor told sister Mae she had cancer, she "ain't" been the same. Certain storms in life, like strong narcotics, will transport us to a whole new mental and emotional sphere of existence. Mentally we are messed up and our perspective of reality is altered. The wounds of emotional and psychological abuse leave us crippled   with neurosis and   psychosis. We emerged from these storms in a far away weird and wacky land of Oz, O.Z., O for outside, Z for zone. Many of us are walking around outside the zone of reality, outside the zone of safety, outside the zone of normality. Spiritually speaking many of you have gone far beyond the outer limits and you are walking around in Oz, in O.Z., in a land that is outside the zone of safety because you have not accepted Jesus as your personal Lord and Savior. You dwell in a kingdom ruled by the wizard. You've been struck in the head and battered by the storms of life.

> Like a ship that's toss'd and driven,
> Battered by the angry sea,
> When the storms of life are raging,
> And their fury falls on me,
> I wonder what I have done,
> That makes this race so hard to run,...
> *The Lord Will Make a Way Somehow*
> (Thomas A. Dorsey)

If the storms of life have put you in a strange place and you are searching for a way back home, try Jesus. The Bible says, Jesus is the way, the truth and the Life (John 14:6).

A main focus of the story of the Wizard of Oz centers on the journey and adventure of Dorothy and her three new friends to the greatly feared and powerful wizard to obtain help in their time of need. As it turns out, Dorothy went looking in the wrong place and petition the wrong source of power for help. She had the power needed to get back home within her presence all the time.

You know we often go to the wrong place and petition the wrong source of power for help in our time of need not knowing that all the power we need is already within our presence. The Bible says that God is not far (Matt. 7:7 cf Acts 17:27; Jer. 29:13). The Bible says God is a very present help in a time of need (Ps. 46:1). We mistakenly look to the hills, the psychic hotline, the lottery, and go to séances, palm readers, astrologist, spiritual channels, religious fanatics, religious cults, petition ancestors and other idol gods and forget that our strength comes from the Lord (Ps. 121:1-2). We must stay clear of sources of help that rely on the powers of darkness, that rely on demonic and satanic forces of witchery and wizardry.

According to the story, the great wizard of Oz turned out to be a great hoax, a master of deception. Though the wizard appeared to be an enormous and great being, he was actually a small and frail being who used trickery and illusions to create fear in the hearts and minds of men and women. Though he purported to have great power, his power was very limited. This wizard was perpetrating a fraud. Like The Great Houdini, this wizard was a great magician. Like Felix the Cat, he was a small creature with a big bag of tricks. In the story, the great wizard was a great pretender.

Today I want to draw your attention to another wizard. You might say, he's *The Greatest Wizard of All*. I want to expose the truth about this devious and devilish wizard to all people living in the bondage of fear and darkness outside the zone of where the dew drops of God's liberating, soul saving, mercy shine bright. The wizard I'm taking about has many names, many aliases. The Bible calls this wizard **Lucifer** (Son of the morning - Isa. 14:12), but he is also known as (a.k.a.): **Satan** (Adversary - Job 1); **Beelzebub** (Matt. 12:24); **Belial** (Worthless - 2 Cor. 6:15); **The Devil** (Accuser or slander - 1 Pet. 5:8); **The Deceiver** (Rev. 12:9 cf Rev. 20:10); **The Father of Lies** (Jn 8:44); **The Tempter** (Mt. 4:3); **The Murderer** (John 8:44); **The Enemy** (Matt. 13:39); **The Evil One** (Matt. 13:39); **The Wicked One** (Matt. 13:19; Eph 6:16); **The Roaring Lion**

(1 Pet. 5:8; 2 Tim 4:17); **The Great Dragon** (Rev. 12:9; 13); **The Snake** (Gen. 3); **The Serpent of Old** (Rev. 12:9); **The Angel of Light** (2 Cor. 11:13); **The Prince of the Power of the Air** (Eph. 2); **The god of this World** (2 Cor. 4:4 cf. 1 John 5:20); **Ruler of this World** (John 17); and, **The One Who Sinned From the Beginning** (1 John 3:8). Like the Wizard of Oz in the story who was a deceiver, a little man with a big ego who played on the fear and ignorance of his subjects, the devil, is also a great pretender who plays on the fear and ignorance his subjects. The devil is **The Great Pretender, The Greatest Wizard of All**. God allows and permits satan to have some power at some times but God has All Power and remains in control All the time! The devil is nothing but a real life Wizard of Oz.

The devil hates us and works on the basis of ignorance, darkness, deceit, lies, falsehoods, facades, cunning, deception, and guile. A favorite and effective weapon used by the devil is manipulation of truth. He will use a bit of truth and circumstantial evidence to bait us into believing a lie. A good rumor contains an ounce of truth. The Bible says Jesus is the true light which gives light to every man who comes into the world (John 1:9) and in him there is no darkness at all (1 John 1:5). The devil practices evil and hates the light and does not come to the light, lest his deeds should be exposed.

When we put on the whole armor of God we can better defend ourselves as God exposes the enemy to us. We must also arm ourselves with the word of God to fight the devil. For example you may know that the Bible says that the devil **walks** about like a roaring lion seeking whom he may devour (1 Pet. 5: 8) but the Bible also says the eyes of the Lord **run** to and fro throughout the whole earth, to show Himself strong on behalf of those whose heart is loyal to Him.... (2 Chr. 16:9). The devil walks but the Lord runs!

The Lord will always get to you before the devil. If satan is bothering you, you need to know that the Lord is already with you and prepared to show himself strong on your behalf. The devil is a defeated foe. Remind satan of his future (Rev. 20:10). God's promises are true, the devil is a liar. Greater is he that is in you than he that is in this world (1 John 4:4). Read it. As a child of God, you have power. His word and Spirit will guide your footsteps like ruby slippers on a yellow brick road to that great city in the sky and direct you safely home to your heavenly mansion.

Don't let satan rob you of what is yours with perverted truth and weapons of make-belief. Renew your mind with the word of God (Rom. 12:1-2 cf Eph. 4:23; 2 Tim. 3:16-17). You are a soldier fighting in a battle that's already been fought, you're a runner running in a race that's already been won. Be not discouraged. God has not given us a spirit of fear but of power (2 Tim. 1:7) and His word as a weapon to slay the dragon and expose the wizardry of satan.

How do we used the word as a weapon? Let me show you:

satan, the wizard of this world says... / **God's Word says...**

1. *(satan)* You're have a sin sick soul / *(God's Word)* **By His stripes you're healed** (Is. 53:5).
2. You're empty/ **With His Spirit you're filled** (Eph. 5:18).
3. You're broke/ **He'll supply your every need** (Phil. 4:19).
4. You're hungry/ **Your hungry soul I'll feed** (Jn. 6:48,51).

5. You're nothing/ **You're the righteousness of God in Christ** (2 Cor. 5:21).

6. You can't do nothing/ **You can do all things through Christ who strengthens you** (Phil. 4:13).

7. If you're meek you're weak/ **Blessed are the meek for they shall inherit the Earth** (Matt. 5:5).

8. You will die/ **You have eternal life in Jesus Christ** (1 Jn 5:11-12).

9. You are a looser/ **You're more than a conqueror through Christ who loved you** (Rom. 8:37).

10. You have no taste/ **You're the salt of the Earth** (Matt. 5:13).

11. The world don't need you/ **You're the light of the World** (Matt. 5:14).

12. You're life is dark and dreary/ **He who follows Me shall not walk in darkness, but have the Light of Life** (John 8:12).

13. You're parents "ain't" nothing & you "ain't" nothing/ **You're a child of royalty, you're a child of God** (Jn 1:12; Rom. 8:14,15; Gal 3:26; 4:6).

14. He is your friend/ **The devil is your enemy** (1 Pet. 5:8).

15. You're friendless/ **You're Jesus Christ's Friend** (Jn. 15:15).

16. You're lowly job is unimportant/ **You're an ambassador for Jesus Christ, the King of kings and Lord of lords** (2 Cor. 5:20).

17. Nobody wants you/ **Jesus wants you and has chosen and appointed you to bear His fruit** (Jn. 15:16).

18. You're ugly, you're physically unattractive/ **You're body is the temple, the dwelling place of the Spirit of a Holy and Righteous God** (1 Cor. 3:16; 6:19; Jn 14:23).

19. You're unpopular, a misfit and nobody will invited you to be a member of their body/ **You're a member of Body of Christ** (1 Cor. 12:27; Eph. 5:30).

20. You're the same, you'll never change/ **You're a new creation in Christ Jesus** (2 Cor. 5:17).

21. You're a sinner/ **You're a Saint that occasionally sins because you have not been glorified yet - you're not what you use to be and you're not what you're going to be - sanctification is a process** (Eph. 1:1; 1 Cor. 1:2; Phil. 1:1; Col. 1:2).

22. You're environment makes you what you are / **You're His handiwork, God's workmanship, born anew in Jesus Christ to do His work** (Eph. 2:10).

23. You're not a citizen/ **You're a fellow citizen in the Kingdom of God with the rest of God's family** (Eph. 2:19; Phil. 3:20; Eph. 2:6).

24. You're unrighteous/ **You're righteous and holy** (Eph. 4:24).

25. You're enemy your adversary will seek and find you/ **You're hidden with Jesus Christ in God** (Col. 3:3).

26. He can destroy you/ **You're born of God and the evil one, the devil, cannot touch you** (1 Jn 5:20).

27. You're are a member of a race chosen to be salves/ **You're a member of a race of royalty, a royal priesthood, a holy nation, a people for God's own possession** (1 Pet. 2:9,10).

28. You're not loved/ **You're chosen of God, holy, and dearly loved by God** (Col. 3:12; 1 Thess. 1:4).

29. This world is your home/ **You're an alien and stranger to this world in which you temporarily live** (1 Pet. 2:11).

30. You're important, "Mr. Big Stuff & Ms. I Got it all together"/ **You're not the great 'I am' but by the grace of God, you are what you are** (Exodus. 3:14; Jn 8:24,28,58; cf 1 Cor. 15:10).

31. You're incomplete/ **You have been made complete in Jesus Christ** (Col. 2:10).

32. You're an unworthy, sin-sick person/ **You have been justified, completely forgiven and made righteous (Rom. 5:1) You are free from condemnation** (Rom 8:1).

33. You're a sinner by nature/ **You have died with Christ and died to the power of sin's rule over your life** (Rom 6:1-6) **You have been rescued from the domain of satan's rule (Outside the Zone) and transferred into (the zone of) the kingdom of Christ** (Col. 1:13) **You have been crucified with Christ and it is no longer you who live but Christ lives in you. The life you are now living is by faith in the Son of God who loved you and gave Himself for you.** (Gal. 2:20).

110

34. You have no power, no self-respect, no self-discipline/ **You have been given the spirit of power, love, and self-discipline** (2 Tim. 1:7).

35. You've disappointed God and now He don't want nothing to do with you/ **You have been reconciled to God and you are a minister of reconciliation** (2 Cor. 5:18,19).

36. God is ashamed of you and has disowned you/ **You have been saved and sanctified, set apart according to God's doing** (2 Tim. 1:9; Titus 3:5) **Because you have been sanctified and are one with the Sanctifier, He is not ashamed to call you brother/sister** (Heb. 2:11).

37. You have no right to go to God in Prayer/ **You have the right to go boldly before the throne of God to fine mercy and grace in time of need** (Heb. 4:16) **God is our refuge and strength, A very present help in trouble** (Ps. 46:1).

38. You can't get to God without the preacher/ **You have direct access to God through the Spirit** (Eph. 2:18).

39. You don't deserve anything from God so don't even ask/ **You have been given exceedingly great and precious promises by God by which you are a partaker of God's divine nature** (2 Pet. 1:4). **You have received the Spirit of God into your life that you might know the things freely given to you by God** (1 Cor. 2:12).

40. You're guilty/ **You have been redeemed and forgiven of all your sins. The debt**

against you has been canceled (Col. 1:14) You have been established, anointed and sealed by God in Christ, and you have been given the Holy Spirit as a pledge guaranteeing your inheritance to come (2 Cor. 1:21; Eph. 1:13,14). 41. You have no power/ Christ Himself is in you (Col. 1:27) and Greater is He who is in you than He who is in the world (1 Jn. 4:4).

Remember, God's word is truth (John 17:17). The Promises of God are true. Many of us at some time or another have been tricked by satan into believing what we do, how we feel, or what others believe of us makes us what we are. That success equals happiness, that failure equals hopelessness. Wholeness and meaning in life are products of what you have or don't have, what you've done or haven't done. That life's events determine who we are. That we are inferior, that we are losers. Those are lies!

Who you are is dependent upon your relationship to God! Christ has made provision for you to be reconciled back to your heavenly Father. As Christians, we don't serve God to gain His acceptance; we are accepted, so we serve God. We don't follow Him in order to be loved; we are loved, so we follow Him. As a new creation in Jesus Christ you have been delivered from the grip of sin and death. The devil is no longer your master. When you accept in faith Jesus Christ as your Lord and Savior, you are set free. Don't be fooled by the devil. The devil does not have power over any child of God so rise up and walk. Fight the devil with God's word and the Spirit of God that dwells in you. It's time to put on your traveling shoes and walk this road to glory. It's a high way to heaven, walk on up the king's highway. Keep on climbing Jacob's ladder you soldiers of the cross. Step by step, climb the stairway to heaven to receive your crown. The devil can't stop you and his demons can't block you. Stop messing around, its time to make the journey home to be with Jesus. Jesus the Rose of Sharon. Jesus the Bright and Morning Star. Jesus my bridge over troubled water. Jesus, my joy in sorrow. Jesus my hope for tomorrow.

I don't know about you but:

One of these mornings,
One of these mornings,
I'm going to lay down my cross
and get my crown.

One of these evenings,
One of these evenings,
I'm going home to live on high.

Just as soon as my feet strike Zion,
Lay down my heavy burden,
Put on my robe in glory,
Sing and tell the story;

Come over hills and mountain
Up to the crystal fountain,
All of our sons and daughters
Drink of the healing waters.

I'm going to live on forever (Repeat)
I'm going to live forever after a while;
I'm going out sightseeing in Beulah,
March all around God's altar.

Walk and never falter,
Move up a little higher,

Meet the Hebrew children.

Move up a little higher,
Meet the Lily of the Valley.
Feast with the Rose of Sharon.
And it will be always howdy, howdy,
And it will be always howdy, howdy,
And never good-bye.

Will you be watching and waiting?
Will you be watching and waiting?
Will you be watching and waiting?
At the beautiful gate? (Yes! I'll be There!)

And then we'll go sightseeing in Beulah,
March around God's altar,
Walk and never falter.

Move on up a little higher;
See Brother Paul and Silas;
Meet my dear old mother.
Move on up a little higher,
Meet the Lily of the Valley,
Feast with the Rose of Sharon

And It will always be Howdy, howdy,
And It will always be Howdy, howdy,
And It will always be Howdy, howdy,
And never good-bye

Will you be there watching and waiting?
Yes, I'll be there waiting at the altar;
When the angels call the roll in glory
I'll be there.
Move Up A Little Higher (Annie Haley)

REFERENCES

Anderson, Neil T. 1990. Victory over the Darkness:
 Realizing the Power of Your Identity in Christ
Ventura: Regal Books.

THE FOOLISHNESS OF THE MESSAGE PREACHED

Chapter 8

Are You Hungry? Are You Thirsty?

Text: Psalm 42:1-2; John 7:37-39

Background: John 4:13-14; 6:35,48-51,53-58;
                  Isaiah 55:1-2; Acts 17:26-28;
                  1 Thessalonians 5:23; Ps. 107:5-9

Songs: 1. *As Pants the Heart for Cooling Streams*
                  (Old Meter Hymn-Anonymous)
            2. *Blessed Assurance* (Fanny J. Crosby)
            3. *Softy and Tenderly* (Will L. Thompson)
            4. *Is Your All on the Altar?* (Elisha A. Hoffamn)

Main Idea: All humans hunger and thirst for Fellowship
                  with God.

As pants the heart for cooling streams
   When heated in the chase,
So pants my soul, O Lord, for Thee,
   And Thy refreshing grace.

2   For Thee, my God, the living God,
          My thirsty soul doth pine;
       Oh, when shall I behold Thy face
          Thou Majesty Divine!
             Old Meter Hymn (Anonymous)

THE FOOLISHNESS OF THE MESSAGE PREACHED

Prolegomena

All praises to God who is the head of my life. To the ministers, officers, members, visiting friends and guest of this great church. It is indeed a privilege to stand before you as an ambassador of the Lord Jesus Christ and a messenger from God the Father. Least I hold you too long, please turn with me to John 7:37-39. Put a marker there and then turn to Psalm 42:1-2. First we will read Psalm 42:1-2. There it reads,

> As the deer pants for the water brooks, So pants my soul for You, O God. My soul thirsts for God, for the living God. When shall I come and appear before God?
> [Psalm 42:1-2]

Now John 7:37-39 reads as follows,

> On the last day, that great day of the feast, Jesus stood and cried out, saying, "If anyone thirsts let him come to Me and drink. He who believes in Me as the Scripture has said, out of his heart will flow rivers of living water." But this He spoke concerning the Spirit, whom those believing in Him would receive; for the Holy Spirit was not yet given, because Jesus was not yet glorified. [John 7:37-39]

The title of this sermon is in the form of a question. No one can answer this question but you. God's question to you is, *Are You Hungry? Are You Thirsty?*
Pray.

118

ARE YOU HUNGRY? ARE YOU THIRSTY?

Sermon Body

All humans share common traits. Even though you may be of a differing race, different skin color, different dialect, different land, different teaching, different religion, different socioeconomic and political backgrounds, I propose to you that all humans share some common features. Whether you speak French, Portuguese, Vietnamese, Chinese, Swahili, German, Dutch, Spanish, Pig Latin, Jive, Ebonics or the Kings English, I say we all have certain things in common. Whether you a male or female, heterosexual or homosexual, single or married, tall or small, wide or narrow, young or old, educated or uneducated. Whether you dress nice or dress poor, whether you are sophisticated or unsophisticated, whether you have a lot of money or have no money at all, whether you are employed or are unemployed, whether you drive a fancy care or no car, I say we all have some things in common. Whether you are a preacher, deacon, a choir member, an usher, a professional pew sitter, dope addict, or alcoholic, I said it once and I'll say it again, we all share some things in common. The Bible says that we all are born in sin and shaped in iniquity (Ps. 51:5 cf. Rom. 3:23; Eccl. 7:20; Ps. 53:1-3; Ps. 143:2; Ps. 14-1-3; Jer. 17:9). The Bible says, "...*there is not a just man on earth who does good and does not sin*" (Eccl. 7:20). We all fall short of the requirements of a Holy God. We all violate and disobey the statutes and commandments of a Righteous God. You may ask, Why is sin a problem? The Bible goes on to say that, "...*the wages of sin is death....*" (Rom. 6:23). Sin breaks the **Holy Fellowship** we were created to have with our Heavenly Father. Sin separates us from God's lovingkindness and mercy. Sin causes death. That's the problem with sin. You have a problem with sin, I have a problem with sin, we all have a problem with sin.

Another thing that all humans share in common is the mystery of life. We are all mysteriously cast on the sea shore of life. Winds blow. Storms rise. The tide rolls in and the tide rolls out. We confront dangerous toils and snares. We are often thrust into different life situations and circumstances as a result of factors beyond our control. For example we are all born with an inherited sin nature. That's beyond our control. We struggle and fight to survive in this world as we make a pilgrimage through time and space to a place eyes have not seen. Who knows what the end will be? At some point along this journey we stop, we pause, we wonder which way to go, what decision to make, what to do next. We dig in the shifting sands of time for answers to the questions of life. At some point in our struggle to deal with the harsh realities of life we may wonder, Who am I? What is life all about? Where did I come from? When will I understand what I really want out of life? and Why? Why don't I have more will power? Why do I make the same old mistakes over and over again? Why is that *I Can't Get No Satisfaction?* I try, and try, and try, and try, but can't get none. No, no, no satisfaction. Why? Wherein lies the answer? Perhaps the answers to the questions, the vicissitudes, the complexities, the enigmas, the riddles, the Whys?, the How Comes?, the mysteries of life are found in the hands of someone bigger than you or I. Yes, we are all mysteriously cast on the sea shore of life and must journey to a place not made by hands nor seen by human eyes. At some point along this pilgrimage we stop and search for answers that will feed our hungry and thirsty souls. Not only do we all have a problem with sin, another thing we all have in common is the mystery of life.

A third thing we all have in common is that we all experience hunger and thirst. All humans require food and water to survive. Oh, you may not be hungry now but you will be later. You may not be thirsty now, but you will be later. In God's wisdom God created us with biological feedback mechanisms, built-in alarm systems to alert us when we are in need of life sustaining food and water. If God had not installed in us the natural safety devices of hunger and thirst we would become weak, sickly, and eventually die. If you can understand the necessity of food and water for physical survival, then you may find it easier to understand God's message today. God's message for us deals with our hunger and thirst for that which is spiritual. Yes, we all experience hunger and thirst for food and water, but we also experience hunger and thirst for that which is of a spiritual nature. To better understand this spiritual hunger and thirst let us look at 1 Thessalonians 5:23: There it reads,

> *Now may the God of peace Himself sanctify you completely; and may your whole **spirit, soul,** and **body** be preserved blameless at the coming of our Lord Jesus Christ.*
> [1 Thess. 5:23]

When God made man, He made us in His image. God is a triune God. He exists as God the Father, God the Son, and God the Holy Spirit. One God existing eternally in three persons. We also can be thought of as triune beings. That is to say, we consist of three parts. From 1 Thessalonians 5:23 we learn that humans consist of body, soul, and spirit. *"And the Lord God formed man of the dust of the ground, and breathed into his nostrils the breath of life; and man became a living soul"* (Gen. 2:7 KJV). Body, soul and spirit.

The body represents our flesh and consist of the ground from which we where made. Our body consist of all the stuff that we can see, touch, and feel. Our body gives us our physical consciousness and awareness of the world around us. Our body has certain cravings collectively known as the *lust of the flesh*. The lust of the flesh stems from certain physical needs and/or desires. Our body has certain *needs* such as food and water. Our flesh also has certain *desires* such as sex. I hate to burst your bubble but contrary to popular opinion, sex is not a need. You need food and water to survive. You can live without sex. Sex is a desire, not a need. Oh, at times you may feel that sex is a need but you can survive without it so stop hopping in and out of bed with every Tom, Dick, and Harry. You may know a girl named Daisy and Daisy may drive you crazy. You may know a girl named Sue who knows just what to do. You had better leave Floozy Susie and Sick Dick alone. Ask God to cool your furnace down. He will do it and it will do you just fine. We are triune beings. We have a body, a soul, and a spirit. The body represents our flesh. Our body also houses the soul and spirit.

The soul represents our emotions, mind, and will. It gives us our self-awareness and consciousness of our sociological realm. We are emotional beings and we have emotional needs. We have the need for love, joy, and peace. I'm talking about 50/50 love, i.e., the need to give love and receive love in return. We are intelligent beings and we have intellectual needs We have the need to know the truth and be intellectually stimulated. We are creative beings with a free will and we have volitional needs. We have the need to make free and independent choices (Note: Life is full of choices, God *will not* make choices for you, He *will* help you make good choices, He *will* see you through whatever choice you make, but He *will not* choose for you). One reason why we have such a difficult time dealing with issues in life is because of the interplay between our emotions, our mind, and our will. Our emotions may say *Lets Get It On* but our mind may say wait. Our emotions may say, *"Take a walk on the wild side"* but our mind may say, "Don't go there." Our will is constantly being beat down and torn asunder because of the tug-of-war battle between what say the mind and what say the emotions. There are two factors that drive our emotions: (1) the lust of the eyes; and, (2) the pride of life. When you add the lust of our flesh (1 Peter 2:11) with our emotional lust of the eyes and pride of life (1 John 2:16), you have double trouble. The the battle between the mind and the combined forces of strong physical urges that have an emotional attachment often results with the defeat of logic and reason. Yes we have a body and we also have a soul. Our soul consist of our emotions, our mind, and our will. Not only do we have a body, and a soul, we also have a spirit.

The human spirit is not the same as the Holy Spirit. The human spirit can be thought of as the dwelling place of God's Spirit. The human spirit gives us our conscious awareness of God and the spiritual realm of existence. Even though many may claim to be nonbelievers, when tragedy strikes we instinctually call on God for help. The human spirit tells us that there **is** someone bigger than you and I. The human spirit tells us there must be a God somewhere! From within our human spirit resides the hope of deliverance from the problem of sin and the answers to the mystery of life.

Like God, humans are triune beings. When God breathed in Adam the breath of life and Adam became a living soul, God's Spirit entered the human spirit. God's holy Spirit empowered man's will and illuminated man's mind thus enabling man to control the desires of the flesh and emotions. However, when man disobeyed God and sinned, things got messed up and tuned around. Now, because of our inherited sin nature, not only have we lost fellowship with God but we also lost our will power to control the desires of our flesh and emotions. Instead of being spiritually minded and led by God's empowering

Spirit, we became carnally minded, driven by the desires of our flesh and our emotions. We developed depraved and corrupt minds. Our human nature changed from being Spirit filled to being filled with sin. Without the light of God's Spirit dwelling in our human spirit we experience darkness and we suffer violence from the powers of darkness.

God created us with a body, a soul, and a spirit and God created us for a reason. God created us for **HOLY FELLOWSHIP.** *Holy Fellowship* can be viewed as having three dimensions. The **first** dimension of Holy Fellowship is vertical in that God initiates *Holy Fellowship* by blessing us. He invites us to participate in the miracle of life. Though we sin God still wants to dwell in us that we may have life. God sent His son, His name is Jesus. Jesus came that we might have life and have it more abundantly (John 10:10). Jesus offers us abundant life in three ways. Jesus said I have come: (1) that you may know the truth and truth may set you free (John 8:32); and (2) that your joy may be complete (John 15:11); and (3) that you may have peace (John 14:27). In the **second** dimension of *Holy Fellowship* is horizontal in that we choose to bless others in recognition of God's blessings upon us. The **third** dimension of *Holy Fellowship* is both vertical and horizontal in that we bless God with praise (vertical) and a lifestyle (horizontal) that pleases God. It completes the triangle for others will praise God because of your good deeds (Matt.5:16). God made us so that He could have *Holy Fellowship* with us, that is, God wants to bless us and He wants us to bless Him by being a blessing to others and by giving Him praise. Shabach! Hallelujah! Shabach! Praise the Lord!

Herein lies the problem, when the Spirit of God does not reign and rule your life, your life is in a wacky, out-of-sink, disjointed, disconnected, out-of-rhythm, disassociated, muddled, deranged, incoherent, crazy, unbalanced, nutty, insane, messed-up, helter-skelter mode of existence. Your state of affairs is bad because sin has broken your fellowship with God and you have no spiritual power. Your mind is corrupt and your emotional and fleshly desires have a dominant, unchecked influence over your will. You need to have your broken fellowship with God mended so that order will eventually come back in your life, so that the Spirit of God can come into your life with the spiritual power to control your body and soul.

In God's wisdom God created man with a built-in safety feature, a homing device, a sense of void, a sense of incompleteness, a sense that something is missing from our lives. When God created man with a free will, God knew there was the possibility that man would one day choose to disobey God and reject God's Love. When we are out of fellowship with God there is a small alarm that goes off. There is a small voice within us that says something is wrong, something is missing, a groping (Acts 17:26-28), a longing for fulfillment, a desire to be satisfied. This growing hunger and thirst we experience is God's call to come home.

Its like the story of the frustrated old deacon. For many church goers the big meal on Sunday is early in the afternoon after church lets out. Many times when evening comes there also comes a growing sense of hunger or thirst. One Sunday evening this old deacon found himself standing in front of the ice box, staring in it. His wife asked him what do you want? He said, I don't know, I know I want something but I don't know what it is. She asked, do you want some left over food, some roast beef, some baked macaroni & cheeses, some collard greens? No, No, No, I don't want that. How about some pie? No, No, No, I don't want that. How about some cake? No, No, No, I don't want that. I don't want nothing sweet. How about some popcorn,

125

some potato chips? No, No, No, I don't want that. That's too salty. Maybe you want something to drink. How about some juice? I tried that already. No, No, No, I don't want juice. How about some soda? No, No, No, I don't want juice and I don't want any soda. How about some hot tea? No, No, No, I don't want that. How about some coffee? No, No, No, I don't want that. I don't want hot tea, cold tea, or coffee. How about some wine? No! Have you lost your mind? No, you know I don't drink that stuff any more. I don't want that. Do you want some milk? No, No, No, I don't want that. I don't want no milk. Well, what do you want? I don't know, I know that I want something but I don't know exactly what it is? Do you want something hot or cold? Something hard or soft? Something sweet or salty? Something light or heavy? Something to eat or something to drink? What do you want? I don't know, I know I want something but I don't know what it is?

My brothers and sisters, maybe you have been searching for something to fill the sense of void that is growing in your life. God is speaking to you today. You are spiritually disconnected. Food, sex, drugs, clothes, cars, houses will not satisfy your spiritual hunger. Falling in love with Mr. right or Mrs. perfect will not satisfy your spiritual thirst. Becoming a workaholic or a professional student will not satisfy your spiritual void. Getting involved in religious cults will not satisfy your spiritual hunger and thirst. You can not fill the spiritual void that God put deep down in you until you connect with Jesus. Jesus said, *"...I am the way the truth and the life. No one comes to the Father except through me"* (John 14:6). I invite you to put your faith in Jesus Christ as your personal Lord and Savior. For real this time. Totally surrender to Him.

In our scripture, Jesus on the last day of the Feast of Tabernacles cried out to all who thirst to come to Him. The Feast of Tabernacles commemorated the passage of

Israelites through the wilderness and God's provision of food and water during that pilgrimage. However Jesus makes the comparison that just as God supplied their forefathers with food and water necessary for physical life, Jesus offers food and water necessary for eternal life. John 6:35 reads,

> *And Jesus said unto them , "I am the bread of life. He who comes to Me shall never hunger, and he who believes in Me shall never thirst....'I am the bread of life. Your fathers ate the manna in the wilderness, and are dead.....I am the living bread which came down from heaven. If anyone eats of this bread, he will live forever; and the bread that I shall give is My flesh, which I shall give for the life of the world.*
> [John 6:35,48-49,51]

Don't you realize that you hunger for the Bread of Life and you thirst for Living Waters! You are not by yourself. The world is hungry for the Living Bread. Today is a good day to yield Him your body and soul. Oh taste and see that the Lord is good!

When you accept Jesus in your life by faith, its like finally tasting what you been longing and craving. One Christian put it this way,

> Blessed assurance, Jesus is mine!
> O what a **foretaste** of glory divine!
> *Blessed Assurance* (Fanny J. Crosby)

Conclusion

Are you Hungry? Are you Thirsty? Only you can answer this question. Softly and tenderly Jesus is calling. Earnestly and tenderly Jesus is calling, calling, "O sinner, come home!" God is trying to tell you something. Are you Hungry? Are you thirsty? If your answer to the question is yes, then God's message to you is recorded in Isaiah 55:1-2:

> *Ho! Everyone who thirsts, Come to the waters; And you who have no money, Come, buy and eat. Yes, come, buy wine and milk Without money and without price. Why do you spend money for what is not bread, And your wages for what does not satisfy? Listen diligently to Me, and eat what is good, And let your soul delight itself in abundance.*
> [Is. 55:1-2]

Amen!

You have longed for sweet peace
and for faith to increase,
And have earnestly fervently prayed;
But you cannot have rest
or be perfectly blest
Until all on the altar is laid.

Chorus:
Is your all on the altar of sacrifice laid?
Your heart does the Spirit control?
You can only be blest
and have peace and sweet rest
As you yield Him you body and soul.
Is Your All on the Altar? (Elisha A. Hoffamn)

Chapter 9

A Pig's Eye

Text: Matthew 7:21-27; 1 Cor. 3:10-15

Background: Luke 6:46-49

Songs: 1. *The Solid Rock* (Edward Mote)
       2. *In Times Like These* (Ruth Caye Jones)
       3. *Rock of Ages* (Augustus M. Toplady)

Main Idea: Jesus is the rock of the Believer's
              foundation.

Prolegomena

All praises to God who is the head of my life, to the pastor
of this great church, pulpit ministers, officers, members,
visitors and special guests, it is indeed a privilege to stand
before you today as God's messenger. Please turn with me
to Matthew 7:21-27. Then I want you to turn over to 1 Cor.
3:10-15. Matthew 7:21-27 reads as follows:

> *Not everyone who says to Me. "Lord,
> Lord," shall enter the kingdom of heaven,
> but he who does the will of My Father in
> heaven. Many will say to Me in that day,
> "Lord, Lord, have we not prophesied in
> Your name, cast out demons in Your name,*

*and done many wonders in Your name?"
And then I will declare to them, I never
knew you; depart from Me, you who
practice lawlessness! Therefore whoever
hears these sayings of Mine, and does
them, I will liken him to a wise man who
built his house on the rock: and the rain
descended, the floods came, and the winds
blew and beat on that house; and it did not
fall, for it was founded on the rock. Now
everyone who hears these sayings of Mine
and does not do them, will be like a foolish
man who built his house on the sand: and
the rain descended, the floods came, and
the winds blew and beat on that house; and
it fell. And great was its fall.*
[Matthew 7:21-27]

Now turn over to 1 Cor. 3:10-15. There it reads:

*According to the grace of God which was
given to me, as a wise master builder I have
laid the foundation, and another builds on it.
But let each one take heed how he builds on
it. For no other foundation can anyone lay
than that which is laid, which is Jesus
Christ. Now if anyone builds on this
foundation with gold, silver, precious
stones, wood, hay, straw, each one's work
will become manifest; for the Day will
declare it by fire; and the fire will test each
one's work, of what sort it is. If anyone's
work which he has built on it endures, he
will receive a reward. If anyone's work is*

burned, he will suffer loss; but he himself will be saved, yet so as through fire.
[1 Cor. 3:10-15]

The title of this sermon is **A Pig's Eye.**
Pray.

Sermon Body

What is your philosophy of life? A perusal and careful examination of human behavior reflects the syncretism, the blending of conflicting philosophies. When you adhere, or follow, one philosophy one day and switch to another philosophy on another day based on your emotional feelings and which ever way the winds blow, that's the way your philosophy goes, you invite confusion, inconsistency, and havoc into your life. Cognizant and mindful of the of the fact that there may be as many different philosophies as there are people, God's question to you today is, What is **your** philosophy of life? Much observable human behavior and practice is governed by one's philosophy of life, one's philosophy of life is likewise governed by one's world and life view. There are some other forces that effect human behavior but today lets deal with the mind.

The best way to ascertain what your world view and your life view is to ask yourself three main question. How you answer these three questions determines your philosophy of life. Ready?

(1) **What is real?** Question number one deals with metaphysics.

(2) **What is truth?** This second question deals with epistemology.

(3) **What is of value?** This third question deals with axiology.

What is real? What is truth? What is of value? How these three questions are answered delineates major philosophical world views. There are five major philosophical world views that have significant implications in the theory and practice of education:

 (1) Neo-Thomism,
   (a) Rational
   (b) Ecclesiastical (e.g. Aquinas);
 (2) Idealism (e.g. Plato, Kant);
 (3) Naturalism/Realism (e.g, Aristotle);
 (4) Experimentalism/Pragmatism (John Dewey);
 (5) Existentialism (e.g. Bultman, Tillich, Barth).

Heres how I answer these questions,

What is real? *God (the Father, Son and Holy Spirit) and God's creation (the world and all that dwell therein)* (Gen. 1-2; John 1:1-14; Ps. 24:1-2).

What is true? *God's Word (the Holy Bible)* (John 17:17).

What is good and of value? *Faith, Hope, and Love.* (1 Cor. 13:13; Matt. 22:34-40; John 14:21).

If you answer these questions in a like fashion, then you fall in the category of Ecclesiastical Neo-Thomism. Well, you may ask, what does all that mean and why is it of any importance to me?

Your philosophical world view is important because it represents your foundational view of life and your foundational view of life effects what course you will choose in life. It effects how you determine what's important in life. It determines how you value, prioritize, and make decisions in life. Your philosophy serves as a guide as you climb up the rough side of the mountain of life. For example, if your are riding a motorcycle at great speeds and you come to a sharp curve, your philosophy as to whether you shift your weight in or out will effect your ability to safely and successfully maneuver that curve. Likewise, our philosophy of life determines whether we will safely maneuver the sharp curves that we will encounter in life. Because of some faulty philosophies of life many a folk have wiped out on the curve called sexuality and have died with the deadly disease of AIDS.

Live for the moment is not necessary a good life philosophy. Eat drink and be merry is not a good life philosophy. Yes, we must cherish every moment but the philosophy "Live for the Moment" is not a good philosophy. One must consider the future when picking a philosophy of life. There is more to life than what you see and experience. We must look beyond earthly experiences and pleasures when picking a life philosophy.

When picking a philosophy of life we need a " pig's eye." Yes, I said pig as in onk, onk. Jesus tells us to be wise builders as like one who builds his house upon a rock so that when the storms of life are raging, our house will remain standing where we can find shelter in the time of storm. When it comes to picking a world view and philosophy of life, we must be careful to pick one that will withstand the storms of life. Yes we must consider the future when picking our foundational belief system. From the story of the *Three Little Pigs* we learn the valuable lesson of becoming a wise master builder.

As the story goes once upon a time there were three little pigs. Each wet out to build a house. One built a house of straw. Another built a house of sticks. The third built a house of bricks. The first pig, who built the house of straw, finished in no time at all. The second pig, who built his house out of sticks, finished next. The third pig, who built his house out of bricks, labored long and hard. First, this third pig had to find the right spot. He considered a few locations but it took a special eye, a **"pig's eye"**, to find good strong materials and a place that had good soil and bedrock. Before this pig found a suitable place to build, the first pig had finished his house of straw. Before this pig could even start building up from the ground, this pig had to first dig down. In order to build a solid foundation, this pig had to establish anchor footings deep within the bedrock. Before all this was done the second pig had finished building his house of sticks. It took the third pig a long time to build a strong foundation (let me hear you say, "strong") but once this pig's foundation was established, it took no time to complete the job and finish building the brick house.

So it is with us. A wise master builder knows the importance of a building a firm foundation. It takes time to build a good foundation in most anything you do. If you want to do well in school you need good foundational skills, reading, writing, and arithmetic. If you want to go to do well in college you need good foundational study habits. No, you don't study while watching TV. No, you don't wait until the night before the exam to study. Yes, you must concentrate while doing your homework. Yes you must study as you go. If you want a good marriage you must have a good foundational understanding of who your partner is and what your partner is all about before you say,

"I do." Your friends may get married before you, but will their marriage last? If you want to have money you must have good foundational money management skills. If you do not want to be labeled as a menace to society you must have good foundational social skills and respect for law, order, truth and justice.

The story of *The Three Little Pigs* teaches us a very important lesson about building on a firm foundation. For purposes of this message, the houses that the pigs built are representative of foundational or core belief systems. In the story there was a big bad wolf who walked about like a roaring lion, seeking whom he may devour (1 Pet. 5:8). When this adversary came to the house of straw he said, "Little pig, Little pig let me in!" Then he huffed and puffed and he blew the house of straw down. The house of straw did not have a firm foundation. When the big bad wolf came to the house of sticks he said, "Little pig, Little pig let me in!" Then he huffed and puffed and blew the house of sticks down. The house of sticks did not have a firm foundation. The big bad wolf ate the pig that lived in the house of straw. The big bad wolf ate the pig that lived in the house of sticks.

But the pig that lived in the house of bricks was safe. When the big bad wolf came to the house made of bricks he said, "Little pig, Little pig let me in!" And huffed and puffed but he could not blow down the house of bricks. The third pig was a wise master builder. We learn from these pigs that building with hay is not good in the long run. Building with sticks is better, but sticks are not strong enough to enable you to go the distance. If you want to go the distance and see what the end will be, to see the riches that God has prepared for his children, you must build your house on a solid foundation. To become a wise master builder like Paul we must have a pigs eye! Yes, we must eye out good solid Biblically based, Christ centered materials and a place to build our foundational core belief systems that will withstand the wiles of the devil (Eph. 6:11-12) as we press onward to our heavenly abode.

Living in the belief system that says all religions are good and lead to heaven is like living in a house of straw. I got news for you. The winds of God's judgment will blow your house down. Calling yourself a Christian and going to church is better, but guess what, that's not strong enough. You are living in a house made of sticks. The Bible says if you want to see the kingdom of God you must be, got to be, born again (John 3:3). You must have a personal relationship with Jesus Christ and accept Him in faith as your Lord and Savior if you want to be saved. Living within the belief system that acknowledges that God is real, that Bible is truth, and that faith, hope, and love in Jesus Christ is a good thing, is like living in a house made of bricks. If your believe that Jesus is the Son of God and that He died for your sins, if you accept Him as your personal Lord and Savior, than let me congratulate you! You are a wise master builder. Your house is built upon a solid rock. This historically accurate, Judeo-Christian belief system takes into account ones future. This belief system is not only concerned with the hear and now but the ever after. It concerns the eternal well being and safety of the soul. This belief system taps into the eternal wisdom of a magnificent all powerful, all wise, everywhere present God who sits high but looks low (Ps. 138:6 cf. Is. 6:1). It put us into contact with The Fountain of Living Water. It connects us with a faithful God who showers His children with mercies upon mercies each morning there be (Lam. 3:22-23). The God who is, who was, and who ever shall be The Great Emancipator and soul saver.

This belief system puts us into fellowship with the one and only true and living God. He puts clapping in my hand and running in my feet. He eases my doubts and clam my fears. He gives me joy in sorrow and hope for tomorrow. He puts food on my table, thank God I know that He's able. He makes me feel rich when I have no money. He makes me happy when I feel sad. He takes always my hurt and pain. He give me peace in the midst of the storms. Yes, He's is a rock in a weary land, my shelter in the time of a storm.

There's a big storm out on the ocean of life and its moving this old way. Don't you know that it your soul's not anchored in Jesus, you will surely drift away?

> In times like these you need a Savior,
> In times like these you need an anchor;
> Be very sure, be very sure
> Your anchor holds and grips the Solid Rock!

> This rock is Jesus, Yes,
> He's the One;
> This Rock is Jesus,
> The only One.
> Be very sure, be very sure
> Your anchor holds and grips the Solid Rock!
> *In Times Like These* (Ruth Caye Jones)

I don't want you to drift away in to the deep abyss of a burning hell. Have you asked Jesus to come into your life as your personal Savior? Salvation is not based on emotional feelings. You don't have to jump no pews or run down no aisle. You do have to believe in your heart and confess with your mouth that Jesus is the Son of God and God raised Him from the dead (Rom. 10:9). It's a leap in faith. It takes a childlike faith in the Word of God. Jesus is the Son of God and Jesus is the Savior, believe it or not. You can prove it or disprove it with logic but the choice is yours. Make a wise choice. It takes a pig's eye to build a strong house on a solid foundation. Have you spent time surveying the landscape of world religions and philosophies? Have you eyed the right belief system that take into account your eternal destiny and future?

I invite you to consider Jesus today. Right now. Jesus said,

> *...I am the way the truth and the life. No one comes to the Father except through Me.*
> [John 14:6]

Jesus also said, God's Word is truth (John 17:17). And also:

> *Heaven and earth will pass away, but My words will b y no means pass away.*
> [Matt. 24:35]

That's why:

> My hope is built on nothing less
> Than Jesus ' blood and righteousness;
> I dare not trust the sweetest frame,
> But wholly lean on Jesus' name.
>
> On Christ, the solid Rock I stand
> All other ground is sinking sand,
> All other ground is sinking sand.
> *The Solid Rock* (Edward Mote)

You know, Job, like Paul, built his house on the belief in the God of Abraham, Isaac, and Jacob. Job's house withstood the winds of adversity. You know the story, Job was sick so long, unto the flesh fell from his bones. His money, his cattle and children, everything he owned was gone. But Job was able to go the distance.

I have had many tears of sorrow,
I have had questions for tomorrow,
There have been times,
When I didn't know right from wrong;
But through every situation,
God gave blessed consolation,
That my trials come to only make me
strong!

Through it all, Through it all,
I've learned to trust in Jesus,
I've learned to trust in God.
Through it all, through it all
I've learned to depend upon His word.
Through it All (A. Crouch)

That's why I have made up my mind;

I will trust in the Lord,
I will trust in the Lord,
I will trust in the Lord 'til I die;
I will trust in the Lord,
I will trust in the Lord,
I will trust in the Lord 'til I die.
I Will Trust in the Lord
(Traditional African American)

Will you trust in the Lord? Jesus is the Rock of
Ages. No other foundation can be laid than that which was
laid by Jesus Christ (1 Cor. 3:11). I encourage you to read
your Bible daily. The Bible represents good soil and
bedrock and the Bible contains strong building materials.
Establish your foundation in the word of God. Build your
house on this foundation. Build your house on things

eternal, hold to God's unchanging hands. If you do, you like Job and Paul will be able to weather the storms of life and find shelter in the time of need.

Amen.

Chapter 10

The Great Fall

Text: Matthew 19:23-26; Jude 1:24-25

Background : Gen. 18:14

Songs: 1. *Only Believe* (Paul Rader)
       2. *God Specializes* (Unknown)
       3. *Trust and Obey* (John H. Sammis)

Main Idea: God can do the Impossible.

Prolegomena

All praises to God who is the head of my life, to the pastor
of this great church, pulpit ministers, officers, members,
visitors and special guests, it is indeed a privilege to stand
before you today as God's messenger. Please turn with me
to Matthew 19:23-26. Then I want you to turn over to Jude
1:24-25. Matthew 19:23-26 reads as follows:

> *Then Jesus said to His disciples, "**Assuredly
> I say to you that it is hard for a rich man to
> enter the kingdom of heaven. And again I
> say to you, it is easier for a camel to go
> through the eye of a needle than for a rich
> man to enter the kingdom of God." When
> His disciples heard it they were exceedingly*

amazed, saying, "Who then can be saved?"
But Jesus looked at them and said to them,
"With men this is impossible, but with God
all things are possible." [Matt. 19:23-26]

With God all things are what? Possible! Now turn over to
Jude versus 24 and 25. There it reads:

*Now to Him who is **able** to keep you from*
stumbling, And to present you faultless
Before the presence of His glory with
exceeding joy, To God our Savior, Who
alone is wise, Be glory and majesty,
Dominion and power, Both now and forever.
Amen. [Jude 24-25]

To Him who is what? Able! When you read these two
Scriptures there are two words I want you to focus on: (1)
Possible; and, (2) Able. With that in mind, the title of this
sermon is **The Great Fall.**
  Pray.

Introduction

Stuff happens in life. Sometimes things happen as result of
what we do, or don't do. What we say or what we don't say.
But also, stuff happens as a result of factors that are beyond
our control. Well, what kind of stuff are you taking about
preacher? I'm taking about when things go wrong. When
things get broken. When we are unable to fix something or
restore to its original condition. For example, when a child
knocks over a glass of milk, there is no way of restoring the
shattered pieces of glass and the spilled milk back to its
original condition. It's impossible. There is a stage in the

course of normal human development when its especially difficult for a child to understand and accept this strange concept of brokeness. Sometimes daddy and mommy are not able to fix that which has been broken. Unfortunately some people are not able to jump over this hurdle. Some people grow up believing that mommy and daddy can fix every problem. There is a familiar nursery rhyme from the Mother Goose collection designed to help the child, both small and tall, understand the concept of brokeness. I want to focus in on this nursery rhyme this morning and use it to highlight some spiritual truths.

Sermon Body

The nursery rhyme I want to share with you is none other than, *Humpty Dumpty*. You may recall that the nursery rhyme goes something like this:

> Humpty Dumpty sat on a wall
> Humpty Dumpty had a fall,
> The kings horses and the kings men,
> Could not put Humpty together again.

No, no, no, that's not right. Let me try it again.

> Humpty Dumpty sat on the wall,
> Humpty Dumpty had a **GREAT** fall;
> **All** the kings horses and **All** the kings men,
> Could not put Humpty together again.

Humpty Dumpty had a **GREAT** fall. As a result of this great fall, he was broken. No matter what the highest authority in the land did and no matter what the best technology had to offer, no one and no thing was able to make Humpty whole again. This nursery rhymes teaches children that brokeness is a fact of life and when some things break, no power on earth is able to restore wholeness. This nursery rhyme teaches the limited view that in this life when some things are broken, they can not be fixed. Alas, poor Humpty, we know him well, he should not have sat on the wall, otherwise, he would not have fell.

It is not clear what Humpty was doing up there on the wall. Before you get to critical and judgmental as to why he was up there, maybe he was forced up there as a result of circumstances that were beyond his control. Maybe he was pushed off the wall by a strong gust of wind or the work of evil forces. Maybe he experienced some sort of debilitating physical condition or problem that caused the fall. The story does not go into why he was up there or what actually caused the fall, that's beside the point. The issue at hand was his broken state. Why he was up there is past history. The story deals with the present and future state of Humpty. Spending time and energy on why he was up there would not help his present state. It might be helpful for future generations as an object lesson, but it serves no purpose in the process of helping Humpty Dumpty who lay broken next to the wall.

We are very much like Humpty Dumpty. Thousands of years ago, when the earth was still new, when the first humans lived and moved on the face of this earth, our father and mother, the progenitors of the human race had a great fall and we, their descendants as a result of that great fall now live in a state of brokeness. The factual, historical account of this great fall into sin is recorded in the book of Genesis in the Holy Bible. The evidence of the subsequent universal brokeness is seen everywhere you go. Individual brokeness has caused brokeness in the immediate family, the extended family, and has even caused ancestral and generational curses. Individual and family brokeness has caused social, economic, political, and institutional brokeness. We must live, work and play in environments designed by the powers of darkness to break people down physically, emotionally, mentally, and spiritually. We live in a society that is breaking down. Even to the most causal observer, widespread corruption is the order of the day. The rapid advances in modern technology linked with the rapid decline in morality spells doom! Our society is on the road of total destruction. The day of judgment draws near.

As a result of the great fall into sin the course of human events was forever changed. Because of we ventured outside the zone of God's garden of ease and fell off God's wall of obedience we now experience broken fellowship with God. This broken fellowship with God in our innermost being causes us to experience broken dreams, broken aspirations, a broken sense of self esteem and destiny. This inward brokeness has effected our outward wholeness. I say again the cancerous growth of sin and the brokeness it causes is evident everywhere you go. We have babies making babies with the legal right and/or illegal means to break the flow of life to the unborn child. The disease of sin is breaking marriages and families relentlessly and unmercifully. This deadly disease has even spread to our spiritual and moral leaders and is causing them to stumble and fall into the sticky tar pit of moral decadence and decay. We have Christian leaders who are not Christ centered, who are not Biblically based, and who are not being held Accountable. We live in a society where law makers are law breakers. We have institutionalized immoral, unjust laws that deny equality and promote political, economic, and social oppression. We live in a society where we must fight for the inalienable rights of life, liberty, and the pursuit of happiness. I say we live in a society that has been broken by the disease of sin.

We must be careful not to waste time and energy blaming others for the problems and brokeness evident in our lives. We must instead concentrate on solutions. After we have fallen, and have admitted to ourselves that we have been broken, once we identify what the problem is, spending time and energy blaming and pointing fingers at others does not constitute constructive, productive, beneficial behavior. Now is the time to focus on the solutions. Humpty didn't need a debate about what happened, Humpty needed to be restored. Similarly, we must instead focus our attention on discovering solutions.

Some mistakes are beyond our ability to fix. Some things we can not fix and we must learn to accept that. There is a popular prayer called the serenity prayer: It goes like this:

> God, grant me the serenity to accept the
> things that I can not change, courage change
> the things I can, and the wisdom to know the
> difference.

Now the important thing to note here is that just because we can not change or fix a problem doesn't mean it can't be fixed. Just because we can't fix it don't mean it can't be fixed! Sometime we must rely on the help of others to successfully deal with a broken situation. We must learn to be resourceful, to use the helps and resources that have been made available to us. For example we know that some laws are not just, yet we do not exercise our right to vote and change legislation by getting involved. War was fought for democracy. People died in order for many of us to have the right to vote yet we don't use this resource to bring about changes that individually we can not change but collectively we can. Some of us would rather moan and groan and cause a host of peripheral problems by blowing a lot of hot air, by spending time and energy blaming and fault finding but never actually dealing with the problem head on.

Our brokeness from the fall in the Garden is a problem that we can not fix by ourselves. When man fell into sin in the Garden of Eden the relationship between God and man was broken. We tried to fix the problem but sin had infected our inward parts and no matter how much we cried and tried, we have not been able to fix the sin problem. Sin is an inherited problem. Every human being inherits the problem of sin. It's not based on what you did or did not do, its based on what our parents, Adam and Eve did. As a consequence of their actions, we all live in a state of brokeness. We all have a broken fellowship with our Heavenly Father. Throughout the ages men have unsuccessfully tried to fix our broken relationship with God thorough human efforts. We even tried building a tower into the heavens but even that did not work. There is absolutely nothing we can do to restore this broken fellowship with God. Nothing! This broken fellowship is the root cause of our broken unfulfilled life of pain, misery, and strife. Sin is the primary reason why we live in a broken society and it is a problem that we humans can not fix on our own.

When man fell into sin, a cry went out for help. It rose to the heavens and echoed through golden streets of Zion. The cry made its way up to God's Throne of Mercy. When God heard our cry He said quite and heaven and earth stood still. Then said He the apple of my eye has fallen, I must send help, who will I send, and who will go for us? And without delay Jesus, the son of God said Here am I, send me. So God sent His best, His Only Begotten Son. And God gave very specific instructions to Jesus and explained His plan. He said by grace through faith men and women shall be saved from the power of sin and death.

Then Jesus took off His robe in Glory, stepped down through 40 generations and entered the womb of the virgin Mary to be born of man. He walked on this old dusty earth proclaiming the good news about God's plan of salvation to men and women. And after Jesus suffered, bled, and died for the remission of our sins, He rose from the dead with all power in His hands.

I don't know about you but:

1. I am so glad, Christ died for me;
   way back on, Mt. Cal - var - y.
   They stretched Him wide, and hung Him high;
   blood came stream, 'n down His side.

2. My Jes - us cried, out with a voice;
   bowed His head, by His own choice.
   There was dark - ness, ov-er the land;
   when He died, for sin - ful man.

3. He died with a, thorn crown they made;
   death the price, for sin He paid.
   The stain of sin, His blood did clean;
   whit - er than, ev-er been seen.

4. And all the world, did fear His doom;
   when they sealed, Him in the tomb.
   They laid Him there, and there He stayed;
   in the tomb, no noise was made.

5. But ve-ry ear - ly third day morn;
   He be-came, my strong tow-er.
   Yes ear-ly ear-ly, Sun - day morn;
   JE-SUS ROSE, WITH ALL POW - ER!

6. Power, Power, Power, Power;
   All Power, Power, Power!
   Power, Power, Power, Power!
   All Power, Power, Power!

Jesus has the power to make you whole. He has the power to fix that which has been broken. Jesus has the power to do what no other power, can do. You don't become whole the instant you accept Jesus as your personal Savior, but you will eventually become whole in a glorified state of being. When Jesus comes into your life, he begins the process of making you whole. You won't be completely whole until He is finished working on you. That going to take some time. But He **will** finish the job. He is able to get the job done. As a guarantee of this promise He has given us His Holy Spirit. Without Jesus you will never be whole and you have no hope of ever becoming whole again. After all, it was a GREAT fall. All the efforts of men and women throughout the ages has not brought forth a healing to the brokeness caused by sin. Despite of all the technology that we now possess as a result of years of experimentation and mathematical calculations, despite of the sum total of all intelligence of the most brilliant minds this world has ever known, despite our vast resources, our libraries, our computers, despite the heights of modern technology that has resulted from mankind's greatest achievements in aerospace, medicine, biology, physics, sociology, religion, psychology, political science and industry man has not been able to successfully deal with the universal brokeness that resulted from our great fall into sin.

But there is one who is able. Able. No matter how great your fall, I want you to meet the One who is able. Jesus, Mary's baby, Jesus, the Bright and Morning Star, Jesus, the Alpha and Omega, Jesus the Lilly of the Valley, Jesus, the Rose of Sharon, Jesus, the Lamb of God, Jesus is Able (John 1:29)! Jesus can pick you up turn you around, place your feet on solid ground. Jesus can put the broken pieces back together again. Jesus can make you whole again. Your broken relationship can be mended. Your broken body can be restore in health. With man many things are impossible but with God all things are possible! That's why it is written in Jude versus 24 and 25.

Now to Him who is able to keep you from stumbling, And to present you faultless Before the presence of His glory with exceeding joy, To God our Savior, Who alone is wise, Be glory and majesty, Dominion and power, Both now and forever. Amen. [Jude 24-25]

That's also why the song writer wrote these words:

Are there any river that seem uncrossable.
Are there any mountains that you can't tunnel through.
God specializes in things impossible,
And He can do what no other power, can do.

God specializes, God specializes
God specializes, God specializes,
And He can do, what no other power, can do.
God Specializes (Unknown)

If God is able to create the universe, then surely God is able to create in you a clean heart and a right mind. If God is able to cause the sun to shine, then surely He can be a lamp unto your feet and a light unto your pathway. If God is able to breath life into a lump of clay, then surely He is able to breath new life into your broken relationship. If God is able to give sight to the blind, then surely He is able to give you a vision of the heavenly rewards promised to those who faint not in well doing. If God is able to heal all manner of sickness, then surely He is able to heal your broken body. If the Lord God was able to raise Lazrus from the dead through Jesus, then surely He is able to raise new hope in your life through Jesus Christ. If God was able to turn Saul, a chief sinner, into the Paul, a chief pillar of faith and saint, then surely God is able to turn your life around. If the Lord God was able to command a legion of demons and evil spirits to flee from a crazy man into a herd of pigs, then surely He is able to command demons and evil spirits to flee from your life. If a loving but just God is able to destroy men, women, boys, and girls as punishment for their rebellion against God, then surely God is able to destroy you for your rebellious attitude against the commandments of God. If God is able to do all this, then surely He is able to fix what you broke. If God is able to do all these things, than surely God can do what you thought was impossible. God specializes in doing what no other power can do. God is able to bless us abundantly more than we could ever expect or dream.

Were you sitting on top of a wall? Like Humpty, did you have a great fall? Have your friends and family given up on you. Have the doctors done their best yet you find no rest? God is ready, willing, and able to prove that He is able to pick you up and turn your life around if you trust Him and remain faithful to Him. Guess what? Almighty God, Jehovah-rophe is still in the healing business. What miracle are you looking for today? He is able to perform it. Do you believe that He is able. Only believe, only believe, all things are possible if only you believe.

However, whether He will or will not perform the miracle you want is another matter. Don't forget that it's God's decision, its God's prerogative. Hear me now, just because you believe He is able does not mean that He will do exactly what you ask Him to do. Remember He is still

God and He does what He decides is best. But the Bible teaches us not to hinder the movement of God in our lives (Eph. 4:30) and not to break God's flow of blessings to us (Proverbs 28:13 c.f. 1 John 1:9; Ps. 32.5) by unconfessed sin and the sin of unbelief (Heb. 12:1-2). More often than not God is willing to answer our prayers but because of our unconfessed sins and unbelief we become our own worse enemy. Remove yourself as a hindrance by confessing your sins and putting your faith in Jesus. Then trust God that He will do what is just and right with love, compassion, and mercy. And if God decides not to do things the way you want, I encourage you to remain faithful. Trust and obey Him, there's no other way to be happy in Jesus. God loves you and God knows what is best. Remember, "God is too loving to be unkind and too wise to make a mistake." If you have stumbled and fell, I dare you to put your trust in:

Him who is able to keep you from stumbling, And to present you faultless Before the presence of His glory with exceeding joy, To God our Savior, Who alone is wise, Be glory and majesty, Dominion and power, Both now and forever. Amen. [Jude 24-25]

Amen.

REFERENCES

Reid, III, Frank M. 1993. The Nehemiah Plan: Preparing the Church to Rebuild BrokenLives. Shippensburg, PA: Treasure House/Destiny Image.

Chapter 11

Mirror Mirror in God's Law

Text: James 1:22-25; 4:1-10

Background: Rom. 12:1-2; 2 Tim. 3:16-17

Songs: 1. *Am I a Soldier of the Cross?* (Isaac Watts)
       2. *A Charge to Keep I Have* (Charles Wesley)
       3. *Just a Closer Walk with Thee* (Traditional)

Main Idea: Be doers of the Word and not hearers only.

Prolegomena

All praises to God who is the head of my life, to the pastor
of this great church, pulpit ministers, officers, members,
visitors and special guests, it is indeed a privilege to stand
before you today as God's messenger. Please turn with me
to James 1:22-25. Reading from the New King James
Version, you will find theses words:

> *But be doers of the word, and not hearers
> only, deceiving yourselves. For if anyone is
> a hearer of the word and not a doer, he is
> like a man observing his natural face in a
> mirror; for he observes himself, goes away,
> and immediately forgets what kind of man
> he was. But he who looks into the perfect*

law of liberty and continues in it, and is not a forgetful hearer but a doer of the work, this one will be blessed in what he does.
[James 1:22-25]

Now turn over to James 4:1-10. There it reads as follows:

Where do wars and fights come from among you? Do they not come from your desires for pleasures that war in your members? You lust and do not have. You murder and covet and cannot obtain. You fight and war. Yet you do not have because you do not ask. You ask and do not receive, because you ask amiss, that you may spend it on your pleasures. Adulterers and adulteresses! Do you not know that friendship with the world is enmity with God? Whoever therefore wants to be a friend of the world makes himself an enemy of God. Or do you think that the Scripture says in vain, "The Spirit who dwells in us yearns jealously"? But He gives more grace. Therefore He says: "God resists the proud But gives grace to the humble." Therefore submit to God. Resist the devil and he will flee from you. Draw near to God and He will draw near to you. Cleanse your hands, you sinners; and purify your hearts, you double-minded. Lament and mourn and weep! Let your laughter be turned to mourning and your joy to gloom. Humble yourselves in the sight of the Lord, and He will lift you up.
[James 4:1-10]

154

MIRROR MIRROR IN GOD'S LAW

The title of this sermon is **Mirror, Mirror in God's Law.**
Pray.

Introduction

Most biblical scholars believe that the book of James was written by James, the brother of Jesus, somewhere around 45 A.D. Though the book of James is not placed as the first book of the New Testament, it is generally believed by critics and historians that this book was written early in the first century and was most probably the first New Testament book composed (Gromacki 1974, 339). James addresses this book to Christian Jews who were scattered throughout the Roman empire. Though little is known about the historical background of the writing of this Epistle, the contents of the book suggest that one issue these Christians were dealing with was the problem of moral laxity and poor moral standards (Gromacki 1974, 339). They knew what was right but did not habitually do what was right. Not only was this a problem for them but it is a problem for us. Each generation must participate in the fight against global moral decay and destruction. We also live in a day of moral laxity and poor moral standards. Our society is swimming in an ocean polluted with sin. Though this book was written in a time distant to ours, to a people of a different culture and language, yet, because the Holy Scriptures were written by holy men under the inspiration of an omnipotent, omniscient, omnipresent, immutable, and sovereign God (2 Pet. 1:20-21), this book is relevant and applicable to us and our present state of affairs.

155

Sermon Body

James admonishes us to be doers of the word and not hearers only. There is a blessing in hearing the word of God for Romans 10:13 says:

> For "whoever calls upon the name of the Lord shall be saved." How then shall they call on Him in whom they have not believed? And how shall they believe in Him of whom they have not heard? And how shall they hear without a preacher? And how shall they preach unless they are sent? As it is written: "How beautiful are the feet of those who preach the gospel of peace, Who bring glad tidings of good things!" But they have not all obeyed the gospel. For Isaiah says, "Lord, who has believed out report?" [Rom. 10:13-16]

But there are some Christians who, having heard the good tidings of the gospel message, do not experience God's blessings because they do not obey the gospel nor believe the report of the Lord. The book of James addresses Christians that profess to be Christians but do not live as Christians. Christians who don't talk like Christians and who don't walk like Christians. Christians who honor God with their lips but dishonored Him with their hips. James is saying if we are going to talk the Christian talk, then we need to walk the Christian walk. James is addressing so called Christians who spend their days and nights fighting, lusting after what they do not have, and praying for blessing to satisfy their worldly desires and pleasures. "Oh God, please let me win the lottery. All I want is to buy a new car and a new house. Quite my job. Maybe buy some new clothes. Take a trip. I promise not to act a fool. I'll even give some to the church." Right!

As in the days of James, we are living in a day of moral laxity and poor moral standards. We are living in times where Christian men, women, boys and girls have become lovers of themselves, lovers of money, boasters, proud, blasphemers, disobedient to parents, unthankful, unholy, unloving, unforgiving, slanders, without self-control, brutal, despisers of good, traitors, headstrong, haughty, lovers of pleasure rather than lovers of God, Christians who have a form of godliness but who deny the power of God (2 Tim. 3:1-6; cf. Rom. 1:16). We are slipping in the darkness. We are drowning in the contaminated waters of moral and ethical depravity. We are sinking deep in sin, far from the peaceful shore. We need to be lifted up from the murky waters of lukewarm Christianity. To the casual observer there is no evidence that the behavior of those who profess to be Christians is any different from non-christians and heathens who walk in darkness. Many Christian walk around as though they have been blinded by Satan, the god of this world. True followers of Christ have been called out of darkness into His marvelous light (1 Pet. 2:9). Now we must walk in the light and encourage others to come where the dew drops of God's mercy shines bright. Christians have been commissioned to tell the world, in word and deed, that the Savior has come, that Jesus is the Light, that 's there's is no need to walk in darkness anymore! If you were accused of being a Christian, would there be enough evidence to support the accusation? If you were on trial for being a Christian, would there be enough evidence to convict you?

Not only have many Christians, as individuals, missed the mark but many local churches are not getting a passing grade. Many so called Christian local churches, having sunk to the depths of mediocrity, have kicked Jesus and the Holy Spirit out and have invited the god of this world in. Instead of worshipping the one and only true and living God of Abraham, Isaac, and Jacob they worship the idol gods of a perverted gospel. Instead of accepting God's grace through faith in Jesus, they accept and elevate the notion of Me, myself, and I. Local churches are being run by the "liberated" woman and the modern "self made" man. What a shame. *"Pride goes before destruction, And a haughty spirit before a fall"* (Prov. 16:18). If it weren't for the Lord, on our side, where would we be? What's going on? Have we all gone mad?

Many churches have become social clubs and entertainment centers instead of spiritual hospitals and houses of prayer. The church is a place where the Spirit of God performs *wonder working power* in the wonderful and miraculous drama of the worship experience. How can the local church be effective without spending time in prayer? Much prayer, much power, little prayer, little power, no prayer, no power. Have we forgotten that the church is an institution established by Jesus Christ to do the work of ministry under the direct command and supervision of an all powerful and infinitely wise Holy but Jealous God? What's going on?

In many local churches there is very little actual ministry going on. There is no ongoing evangelism, no ongoing discipleship, no ongoing worship of the triune God, and there are no ongoing compassion based ministries (felt needs based ministry, e.g. small support group ministries). In many churches there is not enough ministry and too much fellowship. Though fellowship can be a form of ministry, unholy fellowship in holy places is not ministry. These unholy fellowships have given birth to improper sexual relationships. Some of these improper sexual relationships have produced illegitimate children. Some of these improper sexual relationships have even spawned the secret modern day worship and sacrifice of unborn and newly born children to the ancient fertility gods of days gone by. The doors of the abortion mill is still open. What's going on?

Unholy relationships in the local church can cause compromise and eventually a breach in the spiritual leadership, government, and economy in the local church. The Church around the world has become a real live soap opera (day time TV) beyond compare. What's going on? God is not happy nor pleased with our present state of affairs. Its time to take inventory. It is time to straighten up and fly right!

There is a story called *The Sleeping Beauty* that aptly describes our condition. Both individually and collectively the Church, Body of Christ, is a thing of beauty that has been lulled to sleep by the cunnings of the devil. Both individually and collectively we need to look into the God's mirror and ask the question, **Mirror, Mirror in God's Law,** reveal the sin that's in us all. We need to look into the word of God to see the true reflection of who we really are. Not only do we see ourselves as we are but the mirror, God's word, speaks to us. Listen to me, God's word speaks to us regarding our true condition. As Christians we need to gaze more often into God's word, God's perfect law of liberty.

Each day when we wake up at some point in the morning we look into some mirror to straighten ourselves up, that is those of us blessed with the gift of eyesight. Likewise we need to look daily into the word of God to check out our spiritual reflection. Do we look like a Christian. Are we dressed like a Christian? Is everything in order and in place. What do you mean in order and in place? Well, have you thanked God for letting you see the light of a new day? That should be one of the first things you do each day. Order. Have you read and meditated on any scriptures today?. The word is a lamp to my feet and light unto my pathway. Order. How can God order your steps if you are unaware of what he has told you to do and what not to do? Order. What I mean by in place? Jesus is Lord, not you. Are you sitting on the throne of your heart or is King Jesus. In place. If you want God to order your steps you need to let Him up front in the position of leadership of your life. In place. We need to check the word of God to make sure things are in order and in the right place. Daily.

Just as we look into the mirror when we wash-up in the mornings, we need to look into God's mirror each morning to wash up spiritually. We may see that we need to add more love here and there in our lives, we may have to wipe criticism and judgment from our eyes. We need to wash our face with some joy, peace, and patience today. We need to brush our teeth with kindness, goodness, gentleness everyday. Don't forget spray our hair with some self control. And don't forget the sweet smelling fragrance of faithfulness (Gal. 5:22). After we are cleaned up then we must dress up with the whole armor of God. After we get dressed we must look again into the word and check to make sure we are properly dressed for defense and, of course, looking good (Eph. 6:13-18).

James says be doers of the word and not hearers only. Doers of the word are those who daily look into the word of God and continue in the things of God. There is application to what is heard. There is changed behavior based on what thus says the Lord. There is obedience to the commands of God. There is belief in the Lord's report. It's one thing to hear the word of God and another to apply it to our lives.

Many a Christian has missed out on heavenly blessings because of a lack of Christian commitment. Yes, we hear of the blessings of God but we have not experienced the blessings of God. Every Easter, Christmas, and Mother's Day, for some every week, we hear the word of God, but we don't do the word. There is a lack of application. With no application, there is no actualization. If you want to cash in on the promises of God you must not only hear the word but do the word. You must activate the preached message of God by incorporating it into your lifestyle.

For example, salvation is a gift of God. By His grace we have the opportunity of being saved. But we will not be saved if we do not accept the gift through faith in Jesus Christ. The blessing, the gift is conditional. To receive the gift we must apply ourselves by accepting the gift. Many of God's blessing are conditional. In order to receive the blessing we must do something.

God is encouraging you to develop a personal devotion time with Him starting today. Set aside some time to read, meditate, and pray. You wouldn't get dressed without looking into the mirror. God doesn't want you to get ready each day without looking into His word of truth.

Not only does gazing into Gods perfect law of liberty reveal to us the sin that's in our life but the good news is that it also reveals the law of liberty. It reveals the path to freedom! Do you wish to be free from the penalty of sin? We are all trapped in a morally bankrupted sin-sick world but there's no need to be enslaved to moral decadence and decay. The world is on a collision course with the Great White Throne of Judgment. You can be free from the shackles of sin and escape the penalty of a conscious tormenting death! Proverbs 16:25 says, "*There is a way that seems right to a man But its end is the way of death*" (Prov. 16:25) **The word of God reveals the path to eternal life. Hallelujah! Praise God! That's some good news (repeat 3X)!** I don't know about you but I'm determined to look into this book, the Bible, God's mirror, God's perfect law of liberty everyday so that can stay on the right path, so I will look good when I step in Glory. Amen. Don't you want to look good when you set your feet in Zion? If you don't want to show up at the Great wedding feast looking bad, than I advised you to check yourself in God's mirror before you check out from this earthly abode.

Not only does God want us to develop a personal daily devotional time, but another application He wants us to make today is to get involved in some ministry or group to make an impact on today's society. Be it on a local, city, state or federal level, get involved. This will allow you to express yourself as a moral Christian. It's the duty of each Christian to join in the struggle to keep the moral fabric of this society from unwinding. Jesus said we are the light of this world and the salt of the earth. We have been given the responsibility. We need to hold up the blood-stained banner. We must lift Jesus up for all the world to see.

While there are numerous problems of living a hypocritical life, let me suggest one last reason why its a bad idea before I conclude this sermon. You are the benefactor when you trust and obey God. You benefit when you live a lifestyle that pleases God. When we do not act like Christians or live the life we talk about and sing about not only do we hamper God's blessing upon others but we rob ourselves of blessings. Even if you don't care about being a blessing to someone else you should at lest care about being a blessing to yourself. Why make the choice to be a hearer and not a doer of God's word? You only hurt yourself when you are unfaithful and disobedient to the Lord. You benefit when you follow Christ, the Lamb of God and remain committed to Him. There is a heavenly pay day on the way.

A song writer once asked the question:

Am I a soldier of the cross?
A follower of the Lamb?

And shall I fear to own His cause,
Or blush to speak His name?
Am I a Soldier of the Cross? (Isaac Watts)

I don't know how you answer this question but my answer
is YES! I am a soldier of the cross, a follower of the Lamb.

A Charge to keep I have,
A God to Glorify,
Who gave His Son my soul to save,
And fit it for the sky.
A Charge to Keep I Have (Charles Wesley)

Yes! We are all soldiers of the cross.
We are soldiers, in the army
We have to fight, although we may have to
cry,
We got to hold up the blood-stained banner.
We got to hold it up until we die.

(1) **My father was a soldier, in the army**
He had his hand on the gospel plow,
But when he died he made it over,
And he don't have to fight no more.

(2) **My Mother was a soldier, in the army,**
She had her hand on the gospel plow,...

Oh we are soldiers, (Lead)
we are soldiers (choir)
In the army,
in the army
We have to fight,
we have to fight,
although we may have to cry.

163

We got to hold up,
    we got to hold up,
    the blood -stained banner.
We got to hold it up,
    we got to hold it up,
Early in the morning,
    we got to hold it up,
We got to hold it up,
    we got to hold it up,
Late in the midnight,
    we got to hold it up,
We got to hold it up,
    we got to hold it up,
When everything go wrong,
    we got to hold it up,
We got to hold it up,
    we got to hold it up,
We got to hold it up,
    we got to hold it up,
And we got to lift Him up,
    we got to lift Him up.
And we got to lift Him up,...
    we got to lift Him up.

Until the day we die,
    we got to hold it up,
    until we die!

Be doers of the Word and not hears only. Amen.

BIBLIOGRAPHY

Gromacki, Robert G. New Testament Survey. Grand
Rapids: Baker Book House, 19974.

Chapter 12

What Have You Been Drinking?

Text: Jeremiah 2:13; John 4:13-14

Background: Jeremiah 3:6-10; John 4:7-37; Isaiah 55:1-3;
               Rev. 22:17

Songs: 1. *There is a Fountain Filled with Blood*
          (William Cowper)
       2. *Near the Cross* (Fanny J. Crosby)
       3. *Room at the Cross for You* (Ira F. Stanphill)

Main Idea: God is the source of living waters.

Prolegomena

All praises to God who is the head of my life. To the pastor
of this great church, fellow ministers of the cross, officers,
members, visitors and guest, it is an honor and privilege to
stand before you as a messenger of God to proclaim the
unsearchable riches of the gospel message preached. The
scriptural text of the message today comes from two
different passage in the Bible, Jeremiah 2:13 and John
4:13-14. First turn with me to Jeremiah 2:13. There it reads,

> *For My people have committed two evils:*
> *They have forsaken Me, the fountain of*

*living waters, And hewn themselves cisterns
broken cisterns that can hold no water.*
[Jeremiah 2:13]

Now turn over to John 4:13-14. There is reads,

*Jesus answered and said to her, "Whoever
drinks of this water will thirst again but
whoever drinks of the water that I shall give
him shall never thirst. But the water that I
shall give him will become in him a fountain
of water springing up into everlasting life.*
[John 4:13-14]

The title of this message is in the form of a question. When
I drop this question into your lap, please don't drop it.
Please don't drop it because its an important question that
God is asking you. The question is, *What have you been
Drinking?*

Sermon Body

The Bible tells the story of Adam and Eve. As you may
recall, over in Genesis 2:16 the Bible says,

**And the Lord God commanded the man,
saying, "Of every tree of the garden you
may freely eat; but of the tree of the
knowledge of good and evil you shall not
eat, for in the day that you eat of it you
SHALL surely die."** [Gen. 2:16-17]

But over in Genesis 3:4 satan, that old devil, that lying
serpent said,

166

WHAT HAVE YOU BEEN DRINKING?

*..."You shall **not** surely die."* [Genesis 3:4]

As the story of Adam and Eve goes, man did eventually eat
of the forbidden fruit and was subsequently kicked out of
the Garden. Ever since man was expelled from the Garden
of Eden men and women have had to struggle for survival.
Ever since that awful day men and women have been
confronted with the frightening reality of death and the
longing desire for life. Thus the end of man's life of leisure
in the Garden of Eden marked the beginning of man's quest
for life as he struggled to survive. The end of man's life in
the Garden of Eden marked the beginning of the slow but
sure process of man's death. To live forever in peace and
tranquillity, surrounded with love and joy without worry
and strife, without death and sorrow is the dream of every
rational living being. Life is better than death. Even though
life may not be all that you want it to be, with life there is
hope for a better day and a brighter tomorrow (x2). Turn to
your neighbor and repeat after me. Even though life may
not be all that you want it to be, with life there is **hope** for a
better day and a brighter tomorrow. Now give God some
praise. Hallelujah!

      With death all hope is gone. Physical death without
Jesus as your personal Savior will commit you to a living
nightmare. Death without Christ will put you smack dab in
the middle of a tormenting, chaotic existence of perpetual,
everlasting existence of agony. With death, there is
increased disorder, increased pain, increased strife and
increased torment with absolutely no hope of relief. For
thousands of years man has viewed death with a suspicious
and doubtful eye. Many people have an unbiblical
understanding of death. Some have taught that death is
peaceful. No, death is weeping and wailing of teeth. Death
is eternal torment as like a lake of fire. No only have many

167

swallowed false teachings about the true nature of death, but there are many nonbelievers who do not believe that they are in the process of dying or will experience true death. *Believe-it-or-Not*, in every generation, there are still many who still believe the serpent's lie, "*You will not surely die*" (Gen. 3:4). Many unsaved folk run around and act as though they will never die the second death. Lord have mercy!

Others asked the question, why must we descend from the thrill and lofty heights of life down into the dark, dreary grave? Why must physical death come as night to disrupt my fun in the sun and rob me from the excitement the light of each new day brings? Why must death rob us of the joy of discovering and experiencing the marvelous mysterious and fascinations and the joys of life.

Why must the body grow old and frail? As a heavy weight sinks in search for the bottom ocean why must the natural process of decay encroach upon us? Why must the sun of my life bow beneath the horizon of death. Why must we loose our hair, our muscle tone, why must wrinkles appear, why must white streaks of hair appear, why must gravity take its toll on us, why can't the appearance of youth, be cast as stone in our lives. Why must I be forgetful. Why must I grow old? Why must my faculties decline just as I begin to understand what life is all about?

If only I knew then what I know now, if only I could turn back the hands of time. Somebody once said, "Baby baby, if I could turn back the hands of time, surely you would be mine", "Surely I would be a millionaire by now", "Surely I would be more advanced in my career."

Is man born to die? From the moment of birth does the process of growth and development necessarily lead to death? Does every man women boy and girl march toward an open grave? Must everyone die? Everybody must go in the valley of the shadow of death one day. Why? Why do some stay here longer than others?

These are just some questions that have entered the hearts and minds of men and women throughout the ages. The nature of these many questions would indicate that life indeed is precious to people of sound mind and body and that it is not unusual for one to spend great sums of money and go to great extremes to prolong physical, human life.

Legends of Eternal Life

Watch what you drink. When we drink something it becomes part of us. Drinking to much alcohol will cause loss of good judgment. When Eve drank the poisonous lie from the serpent's cup of deception, it gave birth to sin and death. When man sinned, not only was fellowship broken with God but it initiated a process called death and awakened man's hunger and thirst for life. Since then men and women have gone to great lengths to conquer death. Take, for example, the famous Spanish soldier and explorer born in 1460. This brave adventurer accompanied Christopher Columbus on his second voyage to America and established a colony on Puerto Rico in 1508. In Puerto Rico he heard a legend about an island called Bimini, where there was said be a spring that could restore youth. Though it is said that this famous 16th century explorer spent a great deal of his life searching high and low for the infamous and elusive *Fountain of Youth*, Ponce de Leon did not find the *Fountain of Youth*. History tells us that Ponce de Leon died in 1521 (Compton's Interactive Encyclopedia, 1993, 1994, *Ponce De Leon*).

History also tells us that others have tried to conqueror death. The legend of the Holy Grail also promised a road to eternal life. The legend of the Holy

Grail is part of the various legends about King Arthur. In this legend's most predominant forms, the Holy Grail is identified with the cup used by Jesus Christ at the Last Supper. In the legends the Holy Grail is the object of a search, and finding it symbolizes a kind of mystical union with God (Compton's Interactive Encyclopedia, 1993, 1994, *Holy Grail*). In a more recent movie version entitled *Indiana Jones - The Last Crusade*, drinking from the legendary Holy Grail produced healing power and eternal life.

Well, what are you taking about preacher? I say ever since man was kicked out of the Garden of Eden man has tried to conquer the grave and the sting of death by way of human effort and initiative. Man has fought death and has vowed to use any means necessary but all attempts have been met with failure. All attempts have been futile.

What is Life Anyway?

What is life anyway that it is so important? After all, isn't life filled with misery and strife? Why not fill our time drinking wine *Grazing in the Grass*. Why not turn life into a *Stoned Soul Picnic*. Why not drown our sorrows and worries of tomorrow with red/yellow honey, sassafras, and moonshine. Isn't that what the Jerusalem visitors thought of the Disciples of Jesus on the day of Pentecost? These devout men from every nation under heaven witnessed the disciples *scurry* down from a Holy Ghost picnic in the upper room. These devout men thought that these disciples were stoned high of some new wine or something (Acts 2:13). People going around speaking in tongues, full of joy and excitement. However they did not realize that from the sky had come the Lord and, with lightening speed, help in the person of the Holy Spirit came rushing into their souls

170

like a mighty wind and as fire to breath life in them and fill their hearts with joy and peace.

When the Spirit of the Lord fills your heart life begins, eternal life, life that goes on and on with our heavenly Father. Life is wonderfully fulfilling. God made us in His image with meaning and purpose but when we are disconnected and out of fellowship with God as a result of our sin, we never experience the true wonder and joy of life. Without God we are merely surviving, our earthly life leads us to an open grave. Everyone is born in sin and shaped in iniquity. Everyone comes into this world separated from God and doomed for eternal death as a result of our sin nature. It's not your fault, you were born with a sinful nature. We all have a problem with sin. However, God has fixed it so that when we accept Jesus Christ as our personal Savior, the sin problem goes away. Sin is washed away by the Blood of Christ. Our broken fellowship with God is mended, we become children of God and as such, we are granted the gift of eternal life and fellowship with the heavenly hosts. With rekindled fellowship with God, there is no second death. Physical death is merely the passage to an eternal utopia, a blissful life free from sin, sorrow, and death. Without Christ, physical death leads one to the judgment of eternal separation from God's love and grace, and confinement to eternal suffering, permanent separation from the warmth and mercy of God. God has given us the opportunity, from the age of understanding to the end of our earthly life, to make the decision to *Live or Let Die*. If we do nothing and *let* things go on the way they are, we will surely die.

Well What Have You Been Drinking?

Death is a reality and there are many different philosophies out there that teach that you can escape death. Ponce de

Leon went looking for a *Fountain of Youth*. Somebody tried drinking a magic potion of herbs and vitamins. Somebody bought expensive oils and creams that promised to restore a youthful appearance. Somebody went looking for the Holy Grail. Somebody called the Psychic hot line to put the aging process in slow motion. Don't you know that there are no charms and no spells that can save you from eternal death. There is but one way. One divinely ordained plan of salvation. You can't get to heaven by being nice. You can't get to heaven by giving money to the church or your favorite charity. You can't go the heaven by learning to speak in tongues. You can't earn your way to heaven. You can't build your way up the heaven.

You can study all the world Religions but don't drink their poisonous philosophies. Don't digest and internalize their teaching. Mohammed may say one thing and Confucius may say another but the Bible says, once you reach the age of understanding, the only way to the Father is through Jesus Christ (John 14:6). By grace through faith we are saved (Eph 2:8-9). It is a gift of God paid by the blood of Christ. To accept Jesus as our personal Savior is to accept the gift of life eternal. You must accept Jesus as your Lord and Savior. Only the Blood of Christ can wash away your sin and present before God in renewed fellowship.

You need to watch what you feed you soul. Just as you are what you eat physical, in a manner of speaking, you are what you eat spiritually. What have you been drinking? There are so many messed up people running around here because we been drinking poison. We've been drinking polluted water and its gotten into our system. What we drinking is killing us. We need to be drinking the sincere milk of the Gospel. We need to feed ourselves with the word of God. We have entered perilous times where men,

...will not endure sound doctrine, but according to their own desires, because they have itching ears, they will heap up for themselves teachers; and they will turn their ears away from the truth, and be turned aside to fables. [2 Tim. 4:3-4]

I know of only one man who was able to conquer death. Through the miracle of modern medicine there have been those who were reported or pronounced dead but who were revived by way of modern medical technology. But they did not bring themselves back from death. The Bible speaks of a few people who, after they died, were brought back to life. But they did not come back to life by their own power but by the man of God working as an instrument of God. But there is only one man in the history of mankind who died, by choice, and raised himself up from the dead. There is only one man who said to death , where is your sting , and to the grave, where is your victory. Jesus Christ is the one and the only one who has walked down into the valley of the shadow of death, kicked open the gates of hell, and set the captives free. Jesus is the only one who was swallowed down into the belly of death and who grabbed the devil, punched him dead in the eye, shacked him in chains of fire, cast him into the jail of defeat, and said move over there's a new sheriff in town! There's only one man that I know that has discovered the right path to eternal life. There is only one man who shines a light, the true light that brightens the path, that lightens ups the King's highway, that reveals the true stairway to heaven's eternal delight. Talk'n about a real afternoon delight.

Cast your lot with us! Join the Christian band. Don't you want to Sign up for the Christian Jubilee! There is no such thing a the *Fountain of Youth* but,

173

There is a fountain filled with blood
Draw from Immanuel's veins,
And sinners plunged beneath that flood
Loose all their guilty stains
There is a Fountain Filled with Blood
(William Cowper)

Conclusion

Ever since man was kicked out of the Garden of Eden man has been searching for a way to regain immortality. Ever since man ate of the forbidden fruit, man has been sentenced to death. For centuries man has tried to regain eternal life but man has not been successful. I have good news today. The Bible talks about eternal life. It gives us the map of how to guarantee a life of bliss and happiness, a life of endless joy that was once available to man but was lost. The Bible teaches us how to get back that which was lost long ago. You don't get it by drinking magic potions of false philosophies. Today so many people, like the sleeping beauty have swallowed the poison of false teachings. Today we have too many sleeping beauties walking as zombies in a slumber to an open grave. Too many of us have swallowed poisonous philosophies as ways to eternal life. **What have you been drinking?** Are you spending your days and nights searching for the Fountain of Youth? Are you drinking the sincere milk of the gospel. Are you studying God's word, fasting, and praying? Do you have a personal relationship with Jesus Christ? Have you ask Him to be your personal savior? What have you been drinking? Amen.

BIBLIOGRAPHY

Compton's Interactive Encyclopedia, Version 2.00 VW Compton's NewMedia Inc. 1992,1994.

APPENDIX

Jesus Rose with All Power!

Calvary's Hill-Ressurection Sunday "Tag"

I am so glad, Christ died for me,
Way back on, Mt. Calvary;
They stretched Him wide, and hung Him high,
Blood came stream 'n down His side.

2   My Jesus cried, out with a voice,
Bowed His head, by His own choice;
There was darkness, over the land,
When He died, for sinful man.

3   He died with a, thorn crown they made,
Death the price, for sin He paid;
The stain of sin, His blood did clean,
Whiter than, ever been seen.

4   And all the world, did fear His doom,
When they sealed, Him in the tomb;
They laid Him there, and there He stayed,
In the tomb, no noise was made.

5   But very ear-ly third day morn,
He became, my strong tower;
Yes early ear-ly Sunday morn,
JESUS ROSE, with ALL POWER!
Refrain:
Power, Power, Power, Power,
All Power, Power, Power!
Power, Power, Power, Power,
All Power, Power, Power!
© 1997 Leonidas A. Johnson

BENEDICTION

Now

may the God of peace

who brought up our Lord Jesus

from the dead, that great Shepherd of the sheep,

through the blood of the everlasting covenant, make you

complete in every good work to do His will,

working in you what is well pleasing

in His sight, through Jesus Christ,

to whom be glory

forever and

ever.

Amen.

[Hebrews 13:20-21]

CRYITAL FOUNTAIN PUBLICATIONI
P.O. BOX 4434
DIAMOND BAR, CALIFORNIA 91765

ORDER INFORMATION

WHAT IS THIS THING CALLED PREACHING?
An Authentic Collection of Sermons
by Rev. Leon Johnson

Authors:
Leon Johnson
Leonidas A. Johnson

PAPERBACK
ISBN: 1-889561-08-8 (Volume One)   Price: $14.95
ISBN: 1-889561-09-6 (Volume Two)   Price: $14.95

HARDCOVER
ISBN: 1-889561-01-0 (Volume One)   Price: $19.95
ISBN: 1-889561-02-9 (Volume Two)   Price: $19.95

THE FOOLISHNESS OF THE MESSAGE PREACHED
An Original Collection of Soul Food Filled Sermons

Author:
Rev. Dr. Leonidas A. Johnson

PAPERBACK
ISBN: 1-889561-11-8 (Volume One)   Price: $14.95
ISBN: 1-889561-12-6 (Volume Two)   Price: $14.95

HARDCOVER
ISBN: 1-889561-04-5 (Volume One)   Price: $19.95
ISBN: 1-889561-05-3 (Volume Two)   Price: $19.95

Note: All prices subject to change without notice. Payable in U.S. funds.

CRYSTAL FOUNTAIN PUBLICATIONS
P.O. BOX 4434
DIAMOND BAR, CALIFORNIA 91765

ORDER INFORMATION

BREAD OF HEAVEN † SONGS OF PRAISE
Daily Biblical Devotional Guide
Featuring Old Meter Hymns, 2d ed.

Author:
Rev. Dr. Leonidas A. Johnson

ISBN: 1-889561-17-7 Hardcover   Price: $19.95
ISBN: 1-889561-15-0 Paperback   Price: $14.95

GO DOWN, MOSES!
Daily Biblical Devotional Guide
Featuring Old Negro Spirituals

Author:
Rev. Dr. Leonidas A. Johnson

ISBN: 1-889561-14-2 Hardcover   Price: $19.95
ISBN: 1-889561-16-9 Paperback   Price: $14.95

Sales Tax: *Please add 8.25% for books shipped to California addresses.*

Shipping: *$4.24 for the first book and $2.17 for each additional book.*

Note: All prices subject to change without notice. Payable in U.S. funds.

CRYSTAL FOUNTAIN MINISTRIES, INC.
REV. 22:17
A NEW MILLENNIUM MINISTRY